AF417482

שיר המעלות
בשוב ה' את שיבת ציון
היינו כחולמים.

A Song of Ascension:
When G-d returned us to Zion
It was as if we were dreaming.
(Psalm 126)

as if in dreams

Notes following Aliyah

Joseph Zitt

Metatron Arts and Media
Herzliya, Israel - Cleveland, Ohio
2019

Copyright ©2019 Joseph Zitt
Published by Metatron Arts and Media
www.metatronarts.com
ISBN: 978-978-965-92742-0-8 (Print)
978-965-92742-1-5 (EPUB)
978-965-92742-2-2 (MOBI)

Edited by Claudia Crowley.
Cover photograph by Janet R. Century.
Cover design by Jessica Prather.
Interior design and typesetting by Joseph Zitt, using KOMA-Script and LaTeX.

To Ḥana Forbes,
my sister,
mentor,
and best friend

Introduction

On November 29th, 2017, when I was 59, I immigrated to Israel from the US. I moved to Herzliya, a city just north of Tel Aviv, along the coast of the Mediterranean Sea. Much of my family already lived there, some in apartments of their own, and some in an assisted living facility that we came to call the House of a Hundred Grandmothers.

Soon after I arrived, I began writing short observations of what I was seeing and experiencing, as well as collecting quotes of what I heard and overheard from people I encountered. It quickly became a daily practice. I posted these observations where friends and readers around the world could see them. This is a selection of what I saw and wrote in that first year of Aliyah.

Monday, January 22nd, 2018 **2:35 PM**

In the train station a soldier, his gun slung behind his back, plays a bad piano well.

Wednesday, January 31st, 2018 9:32 AM

The sign on the bus stop says "Alighting Only." I check my English-to-Hebrew dictionary app to find out whether "alighting" means getting on the bus or getting off.

Thursday, February 1st, 2018 11:55 AM

At City Center, the bus picks up six men in bright pink bunny suits. Most of the suits appear homemade, with varied approximations of bunny faces on the hoods. The men get off at the University railroad station and hop off into the night, chanting a single syllable in unison with each simultaneous bounce.

Monday, February 5th, 2018 **7:32 AM**

7 AM. In front of the all-night grocery, an old man plays *Eli Eli* and *Sakhaki* on a plastic recorder. His hat is at his feet. No one has put anything in it yet.

Monday, February 5th, 2018 9:29 AM

A man in a white shirt and black vest stands in the middle lane of the highway. He waves his leather cap in the air, conducting a symphony of aggrieved honks from drivers who just want to get to work.

Monday, February 5th, 2018 **3:09 PM**

On the steps down to the Wall, a clarinetist plays *La Marseillaise* from sheet music on a wobbly stand. He is more or less in tune with what I think at first is a muezzin, but turns out to be the voice of another musician, vaguely mumbling a song into a mic as he strums an acoustic guitar.

Tuesday, February 6th, 2018 **2:24 PM**

The soldier with the close-cropped beard carries a brown silk scarf draped across his arms, stretched out in front of him.

Wednesday, February 7th, 2018 12:21 PM

"I can tell you are American. You didn't have to say anything. Your spectacles: multifocal. Your baseball hat. Your disorientation coming into Dizengoff. And your beard –" the guard runs two fingers along its contours "–it is goat. Only Americans wear goat beard just like this. So tell me: did you come here to get away from Trump too?"

Wednesday, February 7th, 2018 9:14 PM

I want to say "Because Hebrew apparently doesn't use the Oxford comma, the structure of the statement is ambiguous." But all I can squeeze out is "This... sentence... not... good?"

Friday, February 9th, 2018 **1:57 PM**

The grocer picks up my bag of greens. "Know that these are not –" she says something like *shalev* – "but are instead spinach." This is good, since I don't know what *shalev* means, and I really do want spinach. When I get home, I look up the word and ask some native speakers, but I can't find a relevant meaning. I'm probably remembering some phonemes wrong, which turns what she said into another word entirely.

Saturday, February 10th, 2018 5:04 PM

At the only neighborhood café open on the Sabbath, a tall man wanders in from the patio, staring blankly ahead. He wears a yarmulke and tallit. A cigarette is tucked behind his right ear. Coming back out with a glass of water, he crouches near a low wall at the patio's edge, striking up a conversation with two neatly bearded men seated on the wall.

Monday, February 12th, 2018 **3:59 PM**

At a stand in the shuk, I order *sahleb*. The worker says, in English, "OK, but we say '*sahLAV*'." A few days later, at another stand, I ask for *sahlav*. The worker says "You must mean '*sahLEB*'."

Wednesday, February 14th, 2018 10:53 PM

Dressed in a Harley Davidson jacket and yarmulke, the man silently moves his lips as he stares at the liturgy on his phone. He keeps one arm in the air as he bobs and twists at the sidewalk's edge, simultaneously praying and hailing a cab.

Sunday, February 18th, 2018 **12:14 PM**

Through the windows of the city bus, still dusty after the rain, I am surprised to see sheets of ice on the banks of a creek. Getting closer, I see that they are white plastic, draped over plants, rippling gently in the wind.

Sunday, February 18th, 2018 **4:09 PM**

At the stone table on the boulevard median, a tanned woman leans back on her bench and closes her eyes. A moment later, she opens them, moves her phone from the table to a jacket pocket, then closes them again.

Sunday, February 18th, 2018 4:58 PM

At the red light, a man with a full beard and a parka darts into the intersection and juggles three balls, tossing them high into the air. When the light turns green, he bows deeply, catches the last ball behind his back, and runs back to the curb.

Monday, February 19th, 2018 2:10 PM

The tiny doctor can't reach high enough with her stethoscope, so she hops up onto the examination table to listen to my lungs.

Tuesday, February 20th, 2018 **11:34 PM**

The bus driver drums with his fingers on the steering wheel. The sound would normally be annoying, but he is pounding out a seven-beat pattern, slightly shifting embellishments every time around. Caught up in listening, I almost miss my stop.

Wednesday, February 21st, 2018 4:13 PM

The boulevard is swarming with teenagers, some in parkas, some wearing as little as the law allows. The ones in matching t-shirts all speak English. At the entrance to the market, a gaggle of North Americans gather around women in headscarves seated at checkerboards on the ground. From where I stand, drinking a *sahlab* (it's neither *sahleb* nor *sahlav* here), I watch the women sliding pieces around the boards but can't figure out the game. Another woman in a paisley skirt runs past, weeping and shrieking, waving an empty coffee cup in the air.

Thursday, February 22nd, 2018 11:55 PM

At the Heart of the City, a bus idles at a busy stop. The driver, outside the bus, is checking close to a dozen travel bags, backpacks, and other packages bunched together on the sidewalk. A soldier, his gun slung over his shoulder, stands nearby, talking on his cellphone. Lost or abandoned, a glittering wizard's hat, driven by the breeze, rolls in circles on the ground.

Friday, February 23rd, 2018 1:59 PM

Many of the girls outside today are wearing wide, translucent, multilayered gauze princess skirts and tops. One has flowers sewn between the layers. (Purim is coming.) A princess in a superhero mask jousts with an invisible sword against a boy dressed as Spider-Man. At the curb, six pigeons take surprisingly long to consume a single falafel ball. When they're gone, starlings swoop in for the remaining crumbs.

Sunday, February 25th, 2018 **4:57 PM**

Unused to walking upright, the baby wobbles forward and bumps into the storefront window. She falls, sits up, and laughs. Two large dogs walk up and sit next to her, one on each side. The shopkeeper kneels inside the window and waves. She waves back. Behind her, a boy kicks a kiwi, fallen from a fruit stand, along the sidewalk, abandoning it when it breaks.

Monday, February 26th, 2018 5:31 PM

The passage runs through the ground floor of the building, between the streets at either side. Halfway down, a dozen boys play *Magic: the Gathering*. Three soldiers, two with guns, stand near the window of the Cinematheque, two poking at their phones while the third braids their hair. Down the street, at the corner, a man plays amplified banjo, spooling out fluent bluegrass at the tempo of the clicking of the traffic lights.

Tuesday, February 27th, 2018 5:25 PM

The ground in front of the shop is strewn with oranges, not from a shelf but fallen from a tree on the curb. More zombies than usual shuffle through the office park. Four soldiers, clothes and bodies painted Gumby green, march in lockstep across the street. (Purim is coming.) A hot air balloon in the distance is painted with what I read as grinning stereotypes: Chinese, African, Native American. As it descends, I see that they are really Ninja Turtles. A father and son, fringes flying, play one-on-one soccer in the plaza. Other boys on powered skateboards zoom skillfully around them.

Wednesday, February 28th, 2018 3:00 PM

Sitting quietly in the espresso bar, a man in a tallit and tefillin nods and murmurs, sipping coffee between prayers. A latte costs the same as a shared taxi ride. On the slow city local, I am aware that I'm the only man not wearing a hat and jacket, not wearing black and white. A billboard advertises Passover in Bucharest. I can't read the fine print, but I like the price.

Wednesday, February 28th, 2018 4:01 PM

The main streets are lined with multicolored banners and what I still think of as Christmas lights. The sequence of banners repeats: blue, yellow, red, orange, white. Those that I thought were different are strung east-to-west rather than west-to east. At the café, the server has a strong North American accent. I'm oddly disappointed when she repeats my order back to me in English. Overhead, the speakers play a cover of "Hotel California," overly earnest, with horns.

Wednesday, February 28th, 2018 11:32 PM

The veggie sushi combo is named "Yoko." Colors and textures are like the real thing, but the flavors are new. The restaurant's bathroom is outside the building, across a courtyard and down dark stairs. No lights, but the full moon is enough. (Purim is here.) Taxis hit their brakes and swerve to avoid twin Robin Hoods and a flock of drunken Pokemon. "From this temple of nature," the violinist proclaims, "I emerge with a cigar."

Friday, March 2nd, 2018 **1:55 PM**

"English? Yes. You are from USA? Yes? Citizen in this city? Yes? We are citizens, doing protest. The head of this city, he is building very fast. In a few years, the city will become twice the size. And we need infrastructure, roads, parking. Already it takes me two hours to drive to my work. He says he has plan, but only in December will he say what it is. We need to know now, soon, before elections. Transparency. So Monday, six at night, we will gather in front of city center. We want one thousand people. In Israel, one thousand people is big protest. You will be there? Come, you will see how we do protest in Israel!"

Friday, March 2nd, 2018 2:32 PM

Friday afternoon: At the neighborhood shawarma joint, vats on a long table hold takeout food for the Sabbath. Large men in Yankees and Manchester United t-shirts sneak tastes of some of the food with their hands. I can't tell what any of it is or what it would cost. In the city square, a man with a boom box, fingerless gloves, and dreadlocks sings "Me and Mrs. Jones." A kumquat falls from a tree into my coffee. The coffee doesn't spill. The kumquat is delicious.

Saturday, March 3rd, 2018 **4:37 PM**

A wall of pigeons flies at me in a perfect diamond formation. I am too entranced to flinch. About to collide with me, three of them drop back and over, keeping to the grid as they open a door in the wall. I turn to watch them once they've passed. They return to their formation, ascending as they cross the street. I coo at them in thanks. They don't respond.

Sunday, March 4th, 2018 **12:40 PM**

The giant sea turtle may have died in the rockslide from the nature preserve that changed the textures of the beach. What had been smooth sand, I'm told, is now rubble, sharper and hard to traverse. The dog, finding the body, rolls around, ecstatic, on the turtle's decaying shell. Her human is slightly less thrilled. Even after a cleansing swim at the seaside, she has to give the dog a bath.

Sunday, March 4th, 2018 **10:17 PM**

On the boulevard, between the bike path and the jogging path: two men (one with a beard, one with a shirt) cuddle on a bench, watching football on an iPhone. On another bench, across from them, a woman sleeps, swaddled in dirty blankets. Two runners stop to place fresh fruit and a cardboard box inside the woman's shopping cart. Their dog wanders from the women to the men and back, then follows them away.

Monday, March 5th, 2018 **9:43 PM**

In the dining hall at the House of a Hundred Grandmothers: a simple dance of seats and carts, wheelchairs and walkers. Some eat the common meal as served; some as altered for their needs; some with the help of those, patient and gentle, who sit by their side. At the end, all dishes are stacked, each table's garbage scooped into a metal bowl. Servers circle once again, collecting the remnants, resetting the room for the following meal.

Tuesday, March 6th, 2018 **4:16 PM**

Outside the coffee shop, a man shouts once, gripping his head in his hands, as he stares at a black-rimmed death notice posted, among others, on a municipal bulletin board. In the city square, women in sweaters and scarves sit in wheelchairs beside their caregivers. Men at low tables play rapid-fire backgammon, slamming the markers hard on the boards. I didn't get to do laundry yesterday (nor, due to class, did I get to the protest) and I'm told not to bother doing laundry today – hung out in the dusty breeze, it would only get dirty again. I try to find where, in this labyrinth of storefronts, I might find more socks.

Wednesday, March 7th, 2018 4:45 PM

Great social engineering at this hummus joint: if you bus your own tray, you get free coffee and dessert. A man lies on the ground nearby, jeans torn, smoking hand-rolled cigarettes and singing along with Tom Petty videos on his phone. My shadow moves across those of the perforated bus stop walls, a ghost among the polka dots, crossing cobblestones, Crembo wrappers, and his face.

Wednesday, March 7th, 2018 11:50 PM

"I tell you, you do not want this apartment. We have advertised, but we should not. All around there is construction. You are writer. In the noise it would not be possible to think. And everywhere there is dust. Keep this phone number and call again after a year. Then the apartment will not yet have been rented. Then again you can ask."

Friday, March 9th, 2018 — 12:44 AM

11 PM on the first night of the weekend: from traffic on faraway roads, the rush of distant oceans. Voices from cars parked under a building on stilts still echo, blocks from there. Even fewer storefronts are open than on the Sabbath: a schnitzel joint, a tiny bistro bar, a lone falafel shop. Couples and single people wander past, unafraid; I know of no street crime in this still-small city. Behind too-bright windows, an eternal market never closes. I look inside, enter, and buy an ice-cream sandwich.

Friday, March 9th, 2018 **3:42 PM**

A revelation: prices at the supermarket in the mall are no worse, and some are better, than where I usually shop. Eggs, challah, butter, and cheese are price-controlled. Much of the rest is on sale. (My mother has taught me well.) On the bus home, two teenage girls in matching white t-shirts hug, not holding onto the poles or straps, laughing. They hope their four-footed stance will be more stable as the bus wobbles and turns. It isn't. The overhead display shows a cooler temperature and a different time. Maybe the bus is dreaming of being somewhere else.

Friday, March 9th, 2018 6:07 PM

A screech. A thud. Dogs bark, but stop long before the static drone of the horn. Looking out the window. I see skid marks tracing a small car's journey out of a parking lot and into a tree. Arriving quickly: a volunteer medic (on a three-wheeled motorcycle first used to clear sites after bombings); two EMS workers, putting on their orange vests as they trot to the car; police; an ambulance; maintenance people with chainsaws, cutting down the injured tree. A team shovels and sweeps sand onto oil (either leaked from the car or the cause of the skid). Caution tape blocks the street behind the crash. Just past it, further away than the tree was tall, a man pushes his child's stroller straight down the center of the road.

Saturday, March 10th, 2018 5:14 PM

As I walk farther from my building, the looping echo of a bird call slips out of sync. It isn't one bird but two, going through a Steve Reich phase. A stream of high-pitched babble interrupts them. Turning the corner, I see a woman bouncing a baby in her arms. "Who's speaking gibberish?" she murmurs. "Who? Mama's speaking gibberish!" At a crosswalk, I wait for the sound of the traffic lights. Most click slowly, sharing a hocketed rhythm. When the box to my right clicks more quickly, about seven ticks to each cycle of the others, it's time to cross.

Sunday, March 11th, 2018 11:58 AM

The doctor types rapidly, using all the fingers on her left hand but only one finger on her right. We talk about eating in Israel and in the US. "Yes, it is perhaps too easy to get coffee and a pastry here. When I visited my sister in Brooklyn, in Bushwick – you know Bushwick? – I wanted to get inexpensive coffee and a pastry, but all they had was coffee, coffee, and it was the filter coffee, the drip. Not like here, with the milk and also the pastry. But yes, fewer calories, so that is good." She taps the Enter key. My phone immediately buzzes with SMSes of further appointments. "I will see you again. You will be well."

Sunday, March 11th, 2018 **5:29 PM**

They are almost out of hummus at my usual hummus joint. "I can make you only falafel." He speaks to me in English before I say anything, perhaps remembering me from before. I say "Yes" to everything he suggests. It's a good mix. The bonus: what looks like an eggroll but is filled with soft, sweet cheese. Another customer throws a tantrum when the server can't meet her demands. I glance over at the server. In tandem, we roll our eyes.

Sunday, March 11th, 2018 **8:51 PM**

On the boulevard at night: the median is crowded again, save for the games space. Immaculate astroturf bears graphics for hopscotch, long jump, lawn darts, and something else I can't identify, blobby shapes labeled "sea" and "dry land." No one is playing. On a bench, the person I thought was a woman last week is vaguely awake, sitting up and scratching his grey beard. An electric guitar blares from an apartment far above, tuning up and sounding long tones. Electric bikes and skateboards drone arbitrary intervals, zooming in towards me, then away.

Monday, March 12th, 2018 **5:19 PM**

At a burger/falafel joint in a gas station near the bus stop for what I think is the exhibition center: my burgers sizzle as they are pressed flat in the grill. The worker asks me a question several times. I don't understand. Another customer suggests that he try it in English, but neither knows the English words. He asks me something new, using cryptic hand gestures. I say "OK." The burger is adequate, with no surprises. As I look up at the Ninja Turtles hot air balloon floating nearby, I see my bus go past. There will be another soon.

Tuesday, March 13th, 2018 **3:45 PM**

As the missile sirens sound, I am sitting at an open-air café outside a government building. I know that there will be a drill. It's been all over the media. I want to see what people will do and where they will go. What they do: Nothing. "Why are you standing up? It's only a test." That's dismaying. Missiles have hit the city before. Maybe the evening drill will be different.

Wednesday, March 14th, 2018 6:11 PM

The rainy season appears to be over. The Give-and-Take shelves at the bus stops are sprouting books. On the bus, the RFID card scanners are showing network errors. Some people scan their cards anyway. Some don't. The driver shrugs and waves them all along.

Thursday, March 15th, 2018 6:15 PM

Once, my mental maps of towns were full of record stores. Now, they track available bathrooms. I'm getting to know this area's shopping malls, ubiquitous and pretty much identical. As they have since my teenage years, my inner maps show South as up. I'm as confused by West and East as I am by right and left. "Just remember where the water is," I've been told in several cities. I have no inner dowsing rod. Without actually seeing them, I cannot find the ocean, lake, or sea.

Thursday, March 15th, 2018 **8:38 PM**

Someone's annoying, incessant ring tone (on a xylophone, three ascending major thirds followed by a pause) turns out to be a bird and thus somehow beautiful. A conversation with overlapping rhythms, half in Arabic, half in Russian, combines the voices of unrelated people walking past me, talking on their cellphones. The play of lights and colors on the surface of the street comes from an electric billboard above and behind me, reflected by the sidewalk tiles. A high, slowly oscillating whistle echoes from somewhere in the neighborhood; no longer trying to identify it, I enjoy the sound.

Friday, March 16th, 2018 **1:38 PM**

"Come, sit here. Then you won't be alone and I won't be alone." Next to us, a table of well-dressed people are shouting amicably at each other in French. The woman and I don't say anything further, but we exchange smiles when we leave.

Saturday, March 17th, 2018 **9:55 PM**

"She was one of the Hundred Grandmothers, one of three of us on oxygen. The House had to shut off the electricity for repairs a while ago. They set up a generator in one room, brought the three of us down there, and plugged our compressors in. We spent the night there, along with her caregiver, safely breathing, until the power came back and we could return to our usual rooms."

Saturday, March 17th, 2018 10:13 PM

Everyone at the tables around me in the café is speaking English. One young woman explains to two others (students, I'm guessing, at the local business school) why plagiarism is kinda, like, you know, bad. Men at another table argue about American election law. "That's not just Leninist, that's positively post-Castro!" Unused to the relaxed rhythms of a Sabbath afternoon, they stomp away without ordering. I order my usual (Turkish coffee and focaccia bianca, the cheapest thing on the menu), entirely in Hebrew this time. I still don't understand some of the things the server says, but everything turns out well.

Sunday, March 18th, 2018 **8:31 PM**

"I've been to the US two, no, three times, to Hawaii, San Francisco, and New York. My brother is in San Francisco. He went there when he got out of the Army, to sell products from the Dead Sea. All those places were very different from where I grew up, in Manchester and in the south of England. But tell me: where do the Americans with the actual cowboy accents live? I would love to finally experience a real American hick town."

Monday, March 19th, 2018 **2:12 PM**

Inside an apparently-dying fashion mall by the sea: Half the storefronts are empty. One store that is still hanging on is blasting "Seven Nation Army" really loud. All the conversations I overhear are in North American-accented English or in Southeast Asian languages that I can't sort out. The food court consists of a McDonald's (of course) and a pizzeria. The workers' lunch from the pizzeria is disappointing: something in the salad is on the verge of going bad, and I break my fork trying to cut the calzone. The server speaks to me in English right away. Only mad dogs, Englishmen, and Americans on job interviews go out in dust storm weather wearing business suits. My family texts me to insist that I drink lots of water today. I pick up a bottle at the mall's supermarket before I head out.

Monday, March 19th, 2018 — 9:39 PM

In the Hundred Grandmothers' atrium, two garden gnomes relax on the ground next to a short stone pillar with a ceramic owl. In front of them: a frog. Behind them: an enigmatic statue on a curving base, a question mark practicing its noontime yoga. Spare trees rise from amidst dry leaves. Twin pipes descend from above to bring down water from the open sky. Despite their efforts, much of the ground appears parched. "This year, there were no spring rains," a Grandmother calls out, using a word I only know from Deuteronomy. Across the atrium from the dining hall, ghosts of reflections in the glass between us hover, drift, and fade away.

Friday, March 23rd, 2018 **5:58 PM**

Friday afternoon: a man opens two fresh containers of white cheese and a plastic bowl of sausages and cabbage. He discards their lids and leaves the containers on the ground outside a construction site, probably for the cats. At the center of town, a young woman unpacks a guitar case, places it on the ground, and fills it with totems: a teddy bear, a tube of candy with a unicorn's head, and an inflated Pikachu. When I pass the spot again after shopping, she is gone, but I see her later outside a pizza joint, drinking turkish coffee with a group of older men. In my back yard, shifting layers of bird song are punctuated by the thud of falling grapefruit splattering when they hit the ground.

Sunday, March 25th, 2018 **12:01 PM**

Walking toward an appointment: A woman across the street pauses to draw a heart and write two words that I can't read in the dust on the back of an SUV. Construction slows traffic near a backyard grove of orange trees. A pungent mix of tar and citrus fills the air. A sign on a fruit stand nearby shows items and prices in Hebrew and, in English, the fading words "Black Friday." Getting near the office half an hour early, I pause at the coffee shop with the kumquat tree. I hand the worker far too much money. (I still confuse the words for "eight" and "twenty.") She hands me back the correct change, more than the item actually cost.

Monday, March 26th, 2018 8:18 PM

My first day at the new job: Odd forms to fill out with more than the usual questions. Favorite color? Blue. Favorite food? Ice cream. Favorite movie? *Koyaanisqatsi.* Favorite song? Leonard Bernstein's "A Simple Song." Height and weight? If metric, I have no idea offhand. Garbage carts rumbling above our comfortable sub-basement sound like slightly more distant airplanes. "Is it hot or cold outside? There could be a tornado and we'd never know it." I think I'm going to like this place.

Tuesday, March 27th, 2018 **8:55 PM**

On the bus home: a young couple with seven children squeezes past a soldier with a pink Hello Kitty backpack. The woman runs back to grab a baby bottle that bounces down the steps. Four children sit on two of the seats. The other three squeeze into an unused space, knocking over a wastebasket. Another bus stops. Its driver gets out to confront a van that has sideswiped him. Teenagers selling flags pester drivers stuck on the highway. Another teen in shorts and a faded Phish t-shirt brandishes a lacrosse stick like a staff to part the traffic, miraculously crossing the road without harm.

Wednesday, March 28th, 2018 1:07 PM

Awakened by the sound of water, I stumble through the apartment to an open window. It is actually raining. Later, the flowers in a pedestrian walkway smell sweeter than before. Shopkeepers put their wares out on folding tables. Neat squares of clean cardboard appear on a bench. On the sidewalk, a snail takes over a minute to cross a single brick.

Thursday, March 29th, 2018 **6:29 PM**

The woman takes a long drag from a hand-rolled cigarette, blows out a seemingly endless funnel cloud of smoke, then puts her pollution mask back on. "It's the dust," a friend explains. "Some people can handle any smoke, but not the dust. I hate to breathe it, but the orange skies that it makes are beautiful. Is there this dust in America? I want to see the weather there. I want to see storms in summer, strong rain that is not over in five minutes. And snow. In all my life, I have never seen the falling snow."

Saturday, March 31st, 2018 9:49 AM

In the city square on the day before Passover: Impending rain has canceled the day's music and other festivities, but two people sit on the ground playing interlocking riffs on hand-pans. A young girl hops out of her stroller, runs up to them, and dances. At the hummus joint, on the day when people no longer eat bread but do not yet eat matzah, the pita is replaced by a sweet unleavened roll. Stores have wares for the seder on tables on the street for last minute shopping. Looking inside the one with the largest display, I see that the store mostly sells clocks. I stop in at our family's spice merchant for suggestions on what to get to start a new kitchen. He scoops out blends that he has created himself and carefully tells me how to use each. They cost less than I thought.

Saturday, March 31st, 2018 **1:06 PM**

In the acute care center of the House of a Hundred Grandmothers: I am drafted to lead a mini-Seder. I sing the blessing over wine (since I can still sing so that the whole room can hear), the Four Questions (since I'm the youngest Jewish person in the room), and two other songs. The melodies for those two differ from the ones that I know. I get slightly lost. In the main dining hall, I join my family in leading a fuller Seder. Noticing moments when the residents lose focus, we consider ways to keep momentum flowing. As I walk home, I hear voices from seders at houses around me. At a corner of two quiet streets, the air is filled with voices singing *"Echad Mi Yodeya," "Chad Gadya"* (both to melodies that I know), and settings of several psalms. Entering my house's yard, I see and greet people from the Seder upstairs. I enter my basement apartment and quickly fall asleep.

Sunday, April 1st, 2018 **6:51 AM**

Walking to the bus stop, I hear the bird songs change as the sun rises. Three cats, lined up on a stone wall, munch on walnuts that someone has laid out for them. I kick a fallen orange down the road until it crosses an intersection and is squashed by a car. My bus, through the Industrial Zone where all the startups roost and on to the marina, is nearly empty. It looks like any techies awake at this hour have been up all night.

Most, but not all, of the shops on the main street are open. Most, but not all, of the bakeries and falafel joints are not. They find closing for Passover less difficult and expensive than cleaning and converting everything. Many, but not all, of those that have closed are taking the week to do renovations and repairs. Some stores drape fabric over non-Passover products. Some have separate ice-cream freezers, clearly marked either as "Kosher for Passover" or as "not kosher." The café that I visit for lunch has only a few baked goods on display. Other than those, it makes salads and coffee, serving everything in to-go cups and plates. The salad that I eat should come with a Passover roll but doesn't. Another customer yells at the staff about something that I don't understand. I decide not to complain.

Tuesday, April 3rd, 2018 **6:49 AM**

At dawn, the mini-market is still closed, though lights are on inside. From the window upstairs, news radio blends with the sound of dishes. Carefully listening, I miss my turn and find myself on twisting streets seemingly designed by snakes. I guess at which to take and find myself back on the main road more quickly than I would have walking straight.

Wednesday, April 4th, 2018 **10:42 AM**

An old couple sits in one of the small parks in my neighborhood. Each wears a summer hat and jacket over lighter clothes. It's cool now but will be warm later. On another side of the park, a man with orange-rimmed sunglasses sits side-saddle on an electric bike, typing something long into his phone. Concentric white circles surround a monument at the center. From above, they might resemble a target. They remind me of labyrinths that I've walked.

Thursday, April 5th, 2018 8:01 AM

In the supermarket at the mall, a sudden rumbling startles me. When a shopper pulls a bulb of kohlrabi from the bottom of a sloping display, an avalanche of vegetables cascades to the floor. Many shelves and some entire aisles there are still hidden behind opaque plastic. Signs say (I think) that the goods on them won't even ring up at checkout during Passover. On the bus home, four teenagers, tanned and wearing shorts, sit in pairs of seats facing each other with all their legs entwined. I have trouble telling which feet belong to whom. The problems that they have untangling when one needs to get off suggests that so do they.

Friday, April 6th, 2018 **10:30 PM**

At night, almost asleep, I realize that I need to do one more thing. Walking toward the light switches, I hit an unexpected wall. I stop, look around, and try to get a feeling for where things are. My sense of direction has crashed. Colored lights glow dimly at several points (the blue of a phone charger, the orange of a power strip, the red of what I think is an emergency light), but their placement seems wrong. As my eyes adjust, I see that I am facing east rather than north. I walk, keeping one hand on the wall. The texture changes from stone to velvet when I touch the curtain at the entrance to the bomb shelter attached to my apartment. I turn, take a few more steps, and reach the switches. When the lights come on, I scan the room, wondering what else I might have forgotten in the dark.

Saturday, April 7th, 2018 9:17 AM

"You, you are too nice, too soft, too insecure. If you stay like that, you will not survive. Always the people like us, at the bottom of the chain, we report the problem, try to fix the problem, and everybody thinks that we are the problem. You will have to learn to fight, to insist, to change, maybe not be so nice, so American. After some time, you will become like one of us."

Sunday, April 8th, 2018 **5:54 AM**

Saturday afternoon at the House of a Hundred Grandmothers. A letter from the manager about the acute care Seder: "You help fulfill the promise of the psalm, 'Don't cast me off in my old age.'" Downstairs, workers arrange the dining hall for those who will eat there. For those who will eat upstairs, most workers take carts up in elevators, roll them to the rooms, and deliver the meals; the religious Jewish workers climb the stairs, bringing the dinners in separate bags. I eat with my family in their apartment, join the prayers for the end of the Sabbath, then walk home to prepare for another early morning at work.

Monday, April 9th, 2018 **12:24 AM**

The roar of a motorcycle cuts through the songs of dawn birds as it rolls down a pedestrian-only street. Its rider tosses newspapers over stone walls into quiet yards. Workers resting from building a house look up from a makeshift table. An urn on a battery-powered hotplate boils their Turkish coffee. On this first business day after Passover, shoppers crowd a bakery nearby. They grab fresh bread off the rack as quickly as the loaves are set out. One man emerges, munching a roll, and frees his scruffy dog's leash from a pole. A chihuahua and a bulldog, sitting calmly off leash in shadows, rise and follow them home.

Tuesday, April 10th, 2018 **9:31 AM**

As I walk home at night, I see a water tower that I hadn't noticed before, lit bright green against the dark sky, like an H. G. Wells Martian pointing the way to Oz. The center of a traffic circle now contains three-meter tall artificial daisies in a giant post-Mondrian vase. Cats gather on a pristine white couch left by the side of the road. If it weren't too heavy for me to carry and too wide to get through my door, I would consider bringing it home.

Wednesday, April 11th, 2018 11:13 PM

As I shave, a kitten walks down the stone steps to my basement apartment window and stares. People seem to view cats here as casually sacred, leaving them offerings of food and fresh water. At night, I hear them howl and play. In the morning, I see as many as seven in my yard (though I may count some who run in circles around me twice). When I sit on a low wall to write, cats walk up to me and nudge me. Sensing that I have no food for them but present no danger, they curl up by my side to sleep in the shade or in the sun.

Thursday, April 12th, 2018 **2:29 PM**

Looking at footage of Holocaust Remembrance Day (I slept through the event): The sirens start at 10 AM. All traffic stops. Even on the highway, people get out of their cars and stand silently. I think I see people in motion in the distance, but, zooming in closer, it's just the rustling of flags in the wind. When the sirens end, people get back in their cars and drive again (at least until the next traffic jam). But for that moment, everyone there and people all over the country are joined in unity, in silence.

Friday, April 13th, 2018 **5:47 PM**

Parked cars and trucks block the bus lane in front of the bakery. Their flashers lie about emergencies. The buses that need to stop block the only other lane in that direction. Cars shift into oncoming traffic. Horns honk. Drivers swerve. Eventually my bus arrives. Most of the people who get on the bus with me get off when I do. They talk among themselves in Russian, Arabic, and African languages that I can't place. I don't hear any Hebrew or English. One man, not recognizing me, challenges me when I follow them through the employees' entrance. When I speak, he realizes that he knows me; we had never met in person, but had spoken on the phone.

Saturday, April 14th, 2018 **9:25 PM**

Coming home after dark, I stumble carefully through the yard, around curves and down brief flights of steps without banisters. As I fumble for my keys, a light comes on above me. Someone calls my name. "I saw you walking in darkness and I didn't know why." The man from upstairs steps out of a shadow. He speaks no English, but keeps his Hebrew simple enough that I understand. "You know that you can turn on this light from inside, but there is also this here." We come back to the top of the first staircase. He shows me a switch on a wall and turns it off and on. "It's good that you also know of this one now. I wouldn't want you to be hurt." I thank him and head back to the apartment. Getting down the stairs is much easier now. Several cats that had been watching us duck back into the darkness as I pass.

Sunday, April 15th, 2018 **10:00 PM**

"People here are afraid of Florida. They think it's all alligators and hurricanes. Hell, we party in hurricanes. We eat alligators. I'll tell you, cut them into chunks, put them on the grill, a little cocktail sauce? Nothing else like it in the world, bro. Nothing else in the world."

Monday, April 16th, 2018 **8:23 PM**

At the bus stop: A woman scrolls through a list of bus lines on a poster-sized display and taps an icon for more information. I hadn't realized that the display was a touch-screen. A young couple stumbles past, talking in English: "And it was evening, and it was morning, and we've pulled an all-nighter. That mid-term better be worth it."

Tuesday, April 17th, 2018 **9:33 PM**

The sirens sound as I'm walking home from the House of a Hundred Grandmothers. It's the second of two Remembrance Days, this one for the fallen soldiers of Israel and victims of terrorism. No one else is out on the block-long street. As the sirens start, a single car rolls past me, turns into a hidden driveway, and disappears. Each of the three sirens I hear has a slightly different pitch. As at the Dream House, when I move my head I hear varying mixes of the pitches, plus difference tones and beat frequencies. I stand still, hands behind my back, until the sirens fade. Then I continue walking, through a small park (itself named for a fallen soldier), up some steps, then down my street, remembering to turn the light on as I arrive.

Thursday, April 19th, 2018 **1:33 AM**

The first of the Independence Day fireworks appear just after dark, reflected in an upstairs window. Until I hear popping sounds coming from the wrong direction, I think they are an electronic display. Turning to see the highest of them above a building, I almost collide with one of many young girls chasing each other with cans of spray foam and of something like Silly String. The boys joust with giant inflated hammers. Both the spray cans and the hammers are emblazoned with the Israeli flag. Most of the downtown streets are blocked off for the giant fair. I watch dance troupes on the main stage, but the headliners don't engage me. I prefer the high school rock bands a few streets over, playing songs by Leonard Cohen and Queen. I get what I guess is a candied apple from a stand. After an hour, I give up on ever getting through the shell and carefully place it in an overflowing trash can. My path home is lined with discarded spray cans and the varied detritus of street food. I expect that by dawn it will all be clean.

Thursday, April 19th, 2018 **10:40 PM**

Today, as Independence Day continues, almost everything is closed. I end up at one of the few open cafés, the one that is also open on the Sabbath. The crowd is sparse. A woman sitting in front of me has a tattoo of a tape cassette. Another whom I see in three-quarter view wears a white t-shirt with black lettering. I read "merc" and wonder what the remaining letter might be: y? i? k? h? e? Toward the back, a man I had seen being escorted out of another place sits with a glass of water. His tidy suit jacket is buttoned over a dense mat of curly grey hair on his chest and belly. He moves his lips and gestures theatrically, but I don't hear any sound or see to whom he is speaking. My panini (called simply "toast" here) costs some six times as much as where I usually get them, and twice as much as the hummus plate that I craved would have cost across the square. I chalk the cost up to inexperience and try to enjoy what I have.

Sunday, April 22nd, 2018 12:15 AM

Faux pas: I didn't cover my head during the prayers at the dinner table to end the Sabbath. I didn't even think of it. "That's so American," I'm told. "Any Israeli Jewish man would have grabbed a napkin, at least, and put it on his head." Why didn't I? Each time before, I must have been wearing one of my baseball caps. And, thinking about it, it wasn't clear to me as an immigrant whether even non-religious Israeli Jews would do so. I guess they would. Now I know.

Monday, April 23rd, 2018 **12:54 AM**

I am stuck in a beautiful world of drones and murmurs. Due to an ongoing cold and other recurring issues, most sound around me, other than from telephones pressed against my ear, becomes a vague unintelligible blur. The upside: all of the background music in our lobby at work sounds like Harold Budd. The downside: I have trouble understanding what people talking to me in person are saying. I text my team telling them this and apologize for appearing to be ignoring them. My boss texts back, "As long as you hear what's on the phone, we forgive you."

Tuesday, April 24th, 2018 11:27 PM

I run from the bus stop to the laundry just as the owner – young, devoutly Jewish, and, I believe, Ethiopian – has finished locking the door. (A downside of my apartment: no washing machine or dryer, nor any way to hook them up or dry clothes outdoors.) He sees me, smiles, turns back, and undoes the locks. Inside, he climbs over mounds of laundry in the dark, heading directly for my duffel bag. He retrieves it and brings it out. This is only the third time we've met, but he remembers me. I thank him profusely. "Joseph, right?" he asks in English. I nod. He points to himself and says "Michael." "Thank you, Michael," I say in Hebrew. He picks up his bags and heads off. I run (as quickly as I can carrying a lumpy eight-kilo bag) back to the bus stop, To my surprise, I make my connection home.

Sunday, April 29th, 2018 **1:09 AM**

I feel then see, as I walk past the house in progress on the pedestrian street, that the paving stones have become rougher and less even. Several days before, the stones had been torn up by the workmen, perhaps to install something beneath them. I thought that I had seen a palette of fresh stones, but those may have been used inside the fence. The old stones are back more or less where they were, in the same pattern, but dusted with grit. Further down the street, I find myself momentarily lost. The swath of purple flowers overhead is gone, washed down from their tree and away by the week's torrential rains. Looking down to the end of the block, I recognize the low bollard across the street ahead and how the road widens beyond it. I am a few meters from home.

Sunday, April 29th, 2018 11:19 PM

Near midnight, back-lit bright green plastic behind darker green fenceposts parallel to my path hosts shadows and moiré patterns, images of things not seen. The jet fighter hovering in the haze ahead is the top of an idle crane. A black lozenge of fur lunges at me. I can hear but not see which end is barking. The human at the far end of the leash apologizes and crosses the street. On the sidewalk, other shapes, cryptic in the distance, become broken furniture and other junk left for the morning's large trash pickup. Not moved to take any this time, I walk on by.

Monday, April 30th, 2018 **10:46 PM**

"You're from New Jersey, right? But bits of other places, so I guess you've moved around. I'm from Boston. Worst accent ever. So I've tried to grow out of it, go for more of a general voice, like on TV. So you want a cup or a cone? And you get another scoop with that, same thing or different. I'd go for that one, with the wafers. Pairs great with the Nutella. You been here long? Yeah, I figured less than a year. Your Hebrew when you came in. You'll get the pronunciation down. It just takes time."

Tuesday, May 1st, 2018 10:03 PM

The waiting room seems suspended in time. Mottled beige stone tiles on the walls and floor rest at odd angles against bright orange backgrounds. People in blue tunics with yellow piping and matching yellow pajama pants listen patiently for their calls to surgery. In the distance, a group of women moves along an unseen hallway clapping and singing. Once-modern sculptures on plinths around the room trigger memories of the original Star Trek. Downstairs, in the outdoor café, men in yarmulkes and women in full headscarves eat sandwiches and salads. Overhead, the sound system plays an EDM remix of Johnny Cash singing "Personal Jesus." Someone's multicultural bingo card has just been filled.

Wednesday, May 2nd, 2018 **9:14 AM**

The cashier at the supermarket may be twelve years old, at most. The customer in front of me hands her a 200 shekel note. She opens the cash drawer, squints at the bill, then wanders over to the office window with it, leaving the drawer open. "Mama, what do I do with this?" The woman behind the glass takes it from her, lifts it up to the light to make sure that it's legit, then hands her four 50s. The girl comes back, gives the customer three of the bills, makes change from the remaining one, closes the drawer, and moves on to me. The customer bags her own purchases and heads out, pausing to pet a small dog tethered by the door.

Thursday, May 3rd, 2018 **3:30 AM**

Late at night, I smell smoke wafting in through my basement apartment's windows. Alarmed at first, I remember that it's Lag BaOmer, a holiday marked by bonfires, haircuts, and weddings. (I decided to move here when visiting for a wedding this time last year.) This year, the bonfires are a problem. With the strong winds and dry weather (despite recent torrential storms), too much of the landscape is flammable. The government has banned bonfires in some places and restricted their size in others. Announcements at the House of a Hundred Grandmothers have told their residents, many of whom have breathing problems, to keep their windows shut. Although I enjoy the cool breezes that drift through my apartment, I get up from my bed and close mine.

Saturday, May 5th, 2018 **2:59 AM**

"My thing with Hebrew's the complete flip of yours. I went into the army pretty much right when I got here, and boom. Crash immersion. I got fluent 'cause I had to. Thing is, when I went back to the States for Passover, I had to read something from the Hagaddah at the Seder, and nothing. Could barely read it, couldn't understand it. My parents laughed at me. 'You're so good, so Israeli now, you talk Hebrew, you text in Hebrew, and you can't read this?' Yeah, it's like whole different languages. Hebrew from now? I'm good. But hand me the old stuff and I don't know what's going on."

Sunday, May 6th, 2018 **12:14 PM**

Walking down the hallway at the House of a Hundred Grandmothers, I hear caregivers joking in what I think is Tagalog. In much of it, they are repeating one word in different ways: "Duuuuu-ra... du-RAH... du-du-ra-ra-ra-ra..." They laugh uproariously each time. Later, eating supper with my family, I hear an announcement echoing down the hallway. Between the blurriness of the loudspeakers and the reverberations, all that I can understand are "movie" and "7:30." The announcer is singing about half of what he says and proclaiming the rest with over-the-top enthusiasm. Apparently, from the laughter around me, this too is hilarious.

Monday, May 7th, 2018 **12:55 AM**

In Hebrew class, we wrestle with an essay on a Biblical text. I find it familiar, though it's foreign to others. They stumble over odd brief words that I recognize as labels for a book, chapter, and verse. The old language easily comes back to me, though I haven't used it much in forty years. We look at where texts collide, where forgotten tales peek through the surface of much-told stories worn thin. Who really killed Goliath? If not David, was it this Elchanan? If it was David, who did Elchanan kill? Was it Goliath's brother? Or were he and David one and the same? I picture Elchanan, aged and tired, sitting where his sheep once roamed. "If they want to say it was David, let it be David. I've seen his drama, lived through it from afar. Once I killed the giant, my life grew quiet. Let it stay quiet. If history remembers me, even in a sentence somewhere, that will be fine. If not, I won't care. I won't know."

Tuesday, May 8th, 2018 **1:47 AM**

"Her husband moved into the House of a Hundred Grandmothers first, into the acute care section. After a while, she moved into an apartment upstairs here – but she never told him that she had. He was a difficult person. She would come downstairs to acute care to be with him every day during visiting hours. But she would leave when the hours were over, so she could have some time and space for herself. I sat with them in acute care on his last night here. He was in pain. The ambulance took him to the hospital, and he never returned. But she's still here, and she asked about you today."

Tuesday, May 8th, 2018 **8:16 PM**

A sudden street fair erupts at the center of town. It's Jerusalem Day, celebrating Israel's entry to that city, fifty one years ago. Children fill the square in front of the Great Synagogue. A sound truck blasts recorded music. A drum circle pounds its own rhythms, out of sync with the songs. There are more police than I've ever seen here before. Across the street, tour buses spew seemingly endless torrents of high school boys. My bus, when it comes, can only move a few meters before it has to maneuver around a cluster of police cars. The driver stops, opens the door, and yells at the police: "You guys always block the bus lanes. Don't be stupid!" A cop shrugs. The driver slams the door shut, gestures at the cars honking behind him, then joins the honking, demanding that the traffic light in front of him turn green.

Thursday, May 10th, 2018 **12:50 PM**

At the bus stop: a young woman staring at her phone looks up, seemingly terrified, when another woman asks her if their bus has come. When the other woman asks her again, she bites her nails then darts around to the other side of the plexiglass barrier. A small, dark woman with Coptic crosses tattooed on her forehead and temples chatters excitedly into her hot pink phone in a language that I don't recognize. A raven caws from the roof of the bus stop. An old woman in a parka and heavy scarf seems to be imitating it. I realize quickly, though, that she is calling out *"Kar! Kar!"* – "Cold! Cold!" A girl beside her, dressed in the artistically shredded remains of a t-shirt and shorts, looks up at her in annoyance then returns to poking at her phone.

Saturday, May 12th, 2018 **1:23 AM**

Friday afternoon: Across the street from the library, three floors up, there's a party going on at either an office or a large apartment. Young people wander on and off the concrete porch with bottles. Group singing erupts on occasion, so indistinct in rhythm and pitch that it could be either a football chant or Eurovision. At the spice shop, the merchant writes down the details of an apartment that a customer is trying to sublet. Odds are good that he'll find someone to rent it. At the produce stand, a ragged line has formed at the counter. A customer is taking a long time to decide between two pieces of ginger. The people behind him shout "Make up your mind! The Sabbath is coming!" The shopkeeper finally grabs one piece from him, declares "You're buying this one," weighs it, and rings it up. By the time that I catch the bus home, most of the other people are gone. I see a lot of Metallica t-shirts on the shoppers that remain.

Sunday, May 13th, 2018 **6:23 AM**

I walk into the spice merchant's shop in search of lentils. I don't know the Hebrew word for them, and he doesn't know what the English word means. Once I look the word up on my phone, I see them right in front of me: three large barrels of lentils, green, red, and black. The shop is impeccably clean and organized. Barrels and bins hold beans and dried fruit. The spices themselves are behind the counter in clear plastic drawers with neat labels that I can't read from where I stand. The merchant doles out both the pure spices themselves and his secret specialized blends, weighing the small amounts and packaging them precisely. I buy a scoopful of lentils and a container of date butter. Later, I regret getting only the green lentils and consider returning for the red and black, if only to add more color when I cook up a vat of rice and beans.

Sunday, May 13th, 2018 **9:16 PM**

As I emerge from Hebrew class, I hear people singing with a piano somewhere in the neighborhood. The sound echoes and reflects off the buildings' stone walls. I can't locate the source. Today is the actual Day of the Unification of Jerusalem. (My city celebrated on Thursday because the logistics were easier.) Every radio that I hear seems to alternate "Jerusalem of Gold" with last night's Eurovision winner. It's hard to picture two more disparate songs. Playing each, though, projects a sense of effusive patriotism, so it all seems to fit.

Tuesday, May 15th, 2018 **6:27 AM**

As I get closer to the stage (once I figure out where the stage is), the crowd grows more and more dense until I can't move forward any further. Thousands of people are dancing in the square, celebrating the return of our Eurovision winner. DJs spin a variety of songs including, every few minutes, snippets of the winning hit. Giant screens show the Eurovision performance and a Pride promo. Since all of the music has the same meter and tempo, it blends together seamlessly. I have to leave before the star is scheduled to appear, so I move steadily backward through the crowd. There are fewer people as I work my way through, but I'm continually jabbed by the elbows of people doing the song's signature chicken dance. I don't see a security cordon at the back at first, but it's there, about a block further away than I expected. The music gradually fades into a deep droning beat until it is is eaten by street noise and echoes and disappears.

Tuesday, May 15th, 2018 **10:55 PM**

Another city, another square, another dance: at the Gate of the City, hundreds of people, most of them dressed in white, swirl and step to folk and popular songs. It's an annual local tradition, leading up to the holiday of Shavuot. For the slow songs, the movements are somewhere between a Texas line dance and Tai Chi, progressing in wide gradual circles rather than rows. The faster songs move in similar circles, as people spin with complex footwork that I don't think I'd be ever be able to remember, much less perform. These dancers, much older on the whole than last night's crowd, seem to have learned the dances as children and have the steps hard-wired into muscle memory. Again, I have to leave for work before the dancing ends. Again the music fades, but is not consumed by drones. From the bus stop, I see a couple dancing in the light from a shuttered falafel shop to the rhythms that, blocks away, we still can hear.

Wednesday, May 16th, 2018 10:57 PM

A voice about a meter above me calls out "Hello! Happy holiday!" A stream of bubbles cascades around my head. I look up and see a woman on stilts with bright purple lips and a flowered crown. She sprays suds from a squirt gun into the air. Signs in the square at the heart of the city say "Shavuot Happening" (with "Happening" spelled out in Hebrew letters) and "American Fair." At tables and stands, boys throw balls at tin can ziggurats, toss rings at arrays of Coke bottles, and fling darts at balloons. Little girls with painted faces dance on a stage to "Uptown Funk" and, yet again, the Eurovision winner. Parents take pictures of children with backdrops of Super Mario Brothers and of cows. A man with a blue face and hands poses with a gilded picture frame. Another man, his face painted white and with angel's wings, stands on a podium, waving wands slowly in the air, making even more bubbles. Across the street, on another stage, boys perform a cryptic play about the giving of the Torah. Each holds a photograph and wears a headband labeled with the name of a mountain. At his usual corner, the man with the amplified banjo sings "Five Hundred Miles." His next song has beautiful lyrics that I try to memorize so I can research them online. Later, at home, I remember that I wanted to find them, but the memory of the words is gone.

Thursday, May 17th, 2018 **10:33 PM**

The aisle of the bus is barely wide enough to fit the guitar coming through, widthwise, strapped to an oblivious young man's back. I hope the guitar's cloth case is padded. The people whom it hits wish that their heads were padded, too. The radio on the bus is playing Frank Sinatra songs. A pair of bell tones sounds whenever a passenger wants to get off. Their pitch and, once, their timing perfectly matches the first two notes of the "no, no, no" of Sinatra's "Mood Indigo." By the time I leave, the radio is playing an impossibly mannered version of "Sunshine of Your Love." The sound of the traffic and of night creatures outdoors is a relief.

Friday, May 18th, 2018 **9:56 AM**

White balls of fluff flow across the road in a silent stampede, like tiny tumbleweeds or the final stages of dandelions. I think they're from the flame trees. Months ago, they sprouted brilliant red flowers that burst into color high overhead, then almost immediately dropped off and faded to a disappointed brown. After weeks of just showing branches and dull green leaves, they may be springing to life again. The fluff balls may have blown in, though, from another plant further away. In this strong, straight, hot wind, I find it hard to tell.

Saturday, May 19th, 2018 2:51 AM

Friday morning: a white-haired man with a cane jaywalks across a busy street. Traffic comes to a halt and waits. He moves an inch or two with each step, pausing between them. I expect to hear the usual frenzied honking, but the cars remain silent, except for the music that streams from some open windows. He arrives at our side of the street and steps toward the bus stop. Teenagers get up from their seats to make room. Several buses come and go. When his bus arrives, he tells the person standing next to him, who stands and waves it down. He tries to get on the bus but can't step high enough. A soldier sets her bag down, places her hand under his arms, and lifts him high enough for him to get on. A sign above the first seat on the bus quotes Leviticus: "Before the aged, rise." With only a brief flash of annoyance, the woman sitting there gets up and moves back. The man sits down. The bus moves on.

Sunday, May 20th, 2018 **9:45 PM**

Rather than mustard, the sesame pretzel at this coffee shop comes with small containers of strawberry jam and of butter for dipping. I don't try the butter, but the jam works quite well. As I munch on it and write, a couple getting espresso to go drops two of the complimentary chocolates on my tray. "We won't eat these. Enjoy." Once I'm done with the pretzel, I absentmindedly unwrap one of the chocolates and pop it in my mouth. My teeth feel an unpleasant jolt and I spit it out. I see that I had forgotten the second foil wrapper under the paper one. I unwrap that second layer and, making sure that there are no further surprises, devour the chocolate. It is delicious.

Sunday, May 20th, 2018 **10:48 PM**

On the night after Shavuot, more people are outdoors than usual. (On Shavuot itself, I worked and slept.) I hear large parties in progress behind stone walls on the pedestrian street. Televisions blare from open windows several stories overhead. Three teenage girls zoom past, chattering and laughing, riding electric bicycles on an otherwise quiet block. Boys on different bikes practice fancy maneuvers in the empty ground-floor space of the open-air mall. On a narrow darkened path, I approach a motorcycle facing away from me, revving up a few feet ahead. I stop to let it go first. The driver shuts down his engine to let me pass instead. I walk on, then he follows. Once we get to a wide enough point in the road, he speeds up, darts around me, and heads off into the night.

Wednesday, May 23rd, 2018 **6:29 AM**

The air on this bus tastes of sweat and citrus. The vents howl with a breathy moan, like tuneless monks. Some people on the bus juggle bags of groceries. Others hold backpacks on their laps, happy to take them off for a while. News alerts tell people to carry bottles of water and wear sunglasses and hats, but I see only two or three people who do. In my own basement apartment, I have only put on the heat and air conditioning once, to test them. Insulated by earth and with a cross-breeze from tiny windows overhead, I'm still comfortable. But it's only May.

Wednesday, May 23rd, 2018 8:54 PM

A fistfight breaks out behind me at the coffee stand. Two men have come up and slammed objects onto the counter. "Brother, there's a line!" "I am the line!" "Your mother was always the first in line!" That's when they start swinging. The barista calls out "Guys! Guys!" to no avail. Another woman appears behind the counter and claps her hands once, imperiously. "This shop is closed – until these two asses leave." The two men disappear, leaving their intended purchases on the counter. "Good! We are open again. Next!" I turn, cradling my espresso. At a safe distance, three yeshiva boys (black hats, white button-down shirts, tzitzit), a woman with a sheer blouse and denim shorts, and a young boy with a scooter and a mohawk are watching. Further back, a man in a muscle shirt does one-handed push-ups on the median. His dog sleeps beside him.

Thursday, May 24th, 2018 **10:09 AM**

Standing in line at my usual coffee shop in the early morning, I realize that I don't need more caffeine. I've lost count of how many espressos I've consumed working the overnight, and I would like to sleep today. Instead, I get an "ice limonana," something like a mint lemonade slushie. Since it's morning, I indulge in a large. By evening, they always run out of the large lids. I understand that the supplier is suing the coffee chain and wonder if the lack of lids is a tactic on the part of one side or the other. At the front of the shop, two women talk excitedly in what might be Hindi. A man without a shirt bellows into his phone in Arabic. Pigeons squabble over spilled snacks that look like smaller, beige Cheetos. Overhead, the sound system plays "This Is America," loud.

Friday, May 25th, 2018 **9:56 AM**

Small slugs map silent geometries on the yard's white stucco walls. Their traces chart equations that I think too quickly to understand. Around them, large insects pop in and out of view, punctuating the slugs' movement without altering their path. The backyard cats watch the bugs and slugs from a distance, not quite ready to pounce, but making it clear that if they wanted to, they could. I step quietly past them, my shadow sharp against the floodlit stone. I try not to disturb the cats or bugs. I can't tell if the slugs sense my presence. Barring unintended violence, I doubt that they would care.

"That way you've worked out which hand to use for what in printing the cards? It's just like making schnitzel. What, you've never made schnitzel? OK, you need a wet hand and a dry hand. With the wet hand, you have to take the chicken, dredge it in flour, take it out of there and dunk it in the egg, then take it out of there and dredge it in the bread crumbs. That hand becomes a holy mess. But you do it with only the one hand, so the other stays dry and clean for everything else. I see you work things out like that. You figure out what to place where, facing in which direction, and where you use which hand. It seems obvious to me, doing things that way, but a lot of people don't do that. They just do things whichever way they happen, efficient or not. I don't know that I'll ever understand that."

Sunday, May 27th, 2018 **7:13 AM**

At the House of a Hundred Grandmothers, a worker asks a resident for help with her Hebrew. She knows enough to do her job, but, as a woman caring for women, has only learned the feminine forms of verbs. She wants to know the masculine forms, too, for speaking to and about men. Her family is back in the Philippines. Her work here supports them. Many of the Christian ones gather for worship once a week, at a time when most of the Grandmothers can get along briefly without them. The rest of the time, when I see them, they are gathered near clusters of Grandmothers, keeping an eye on them, or sitting or walking with them, with seemingly infinite patience.

Monday, May 28th, 2018 **4:03 AM**

As I wait for the espresso machine at work to do its job, a man reaches past me and takes a paper coffee cup from the stack. Reaching into a bin I hadn't noticed before, he pulls out a roll of tea bags and counts off eight. He puts at least four spoonfuls of sugar in the cup, followed by all the tea bags, and fills it from the boiling water tap. "That's going to be some really strong tea," I say. He glares at me and growls something in Russian. Cowed, I stand quietly until the espresso machine finishes, making its usual dying-Wookiee noise. I take my cup and slink away.

Tuesday, May 29th, 2018 **6:12 AM**

The display inside the front of the bus is undependable. It often lags for several stops then jumps ahead to show a stop beyond the next. The vocal announcements are mostly accurate. I hear that same announcer's voice everywhere in the media, speaking precise Hebrew, different from how people speak on the street. The video display near the side door shows repeated Windows boot errors. (Everything here runs on Windows. Its frequent error messages are a regular part of the landscape.) In the seat in front of me, a woman eats a cookie from a blue paper bag emblazoned with the word Pillsbury in Hebrew letters and a picture of the Doughboy. To my left, a man calls out to no one in particular, "Sixty dollars to Poland!" Behind me, a soldier speaks on her cell phone in Hebrew-accented English. "I am glad that you are enjoying the peace. It is an interesting world."

Wednesday, May 30th, 2018 **8:06 AM**

At the ice cream shop, everyone is speaking English. I get in line. When I'm next, the old man behind the counter gestures at me. "You next?" I think he says. "A cup of the honey walnut yogurt," I reply. "No, no, no. You pay first. There." He points to a register further down the counter. I follow him to it. "Now," he says. "What you want? Cup? Cone? Large, middle, small?" I pay him for a small cup, then take my receipt and get back in line. The young guy with the scoop sounds North American. "What can I get you?" "Honey walnut yogurt?" I ask. "No yogurt, sorry." "But..." I point to the sign declaring the specials. "Yeah, that sign..." He sighs. "No yogurt." He shrugs. I shrug. I get a cup of black cherry gelato, go back outside, and sit down.

Thursday, May 31st, 2018 **10:46 AM**

The guy in line in front of me at the cheese counter is talking a long time. It's worth the wait, though, since cheese is always cheaper and often fresher straight from the deli. I'm waiting for the cheap cheese. He's getting the more high-end stuff, ten to fifteen times as expensive. He points to various cheeses in the case and asks about them in Russian. The worker takes each out, unwraps it, slices off a bit, and gives it to him to taste. He gets everything he tries. When it's finally my turn, I ask in Hebrew for two hundred grams of the yellow cheese, sliced. The worker pulls it out and says, "It's only nine percent fat. Light." She says "Light" in English, though, come to think of it, Hebrew may have absorbed the word. She slices off the right amount. Rather than just wrapping the whole thing together in butcher's paper then in plastic wrap as usual, she gets fancier. She reaches into a cabinet and pulls out a sheet of clear plastic, stronger than wrap but more pliable than cellophane. She lays one end of it flat on the table, puts one slice of cheese on top, then brings the rest of it down, moving the top of the plastic in a zigzag, placing a single slice of cheese in each fold. She then wraps that in paper and puts the whole thing in a clamshell plastic box. I would have been OK with the simpler wrapping. Maybe she figures that the overpackaging will make it taste richer. I doubt I'd be able to tell the difference.

Friday, June 1st, 2018 **6:52 PM**

Friday morning: The bus is more crowded than usual. A cluster of soldiers gets on at the train station, headed home for the weekend. One, exhausted, places his forearm on the back of the seats in front of him, lays his head down on it, and immediately falls asleep. Another, her gun slung across her back, her sequined phone case and purse by her side, wrestles with an olive-green duffel bag that matches her uniform. A third sits down toward the back then gets up and makes her way forward. Apparently unskilled in the ways of walking on moving buses, she stumbles several times and falls once, into the seat in front of me. She asks the driver something in broken Hebrew with a strong North American accent. I guess that she is, like me, a recent immigrant and, from her voice, quite possibly from New Jersey. At the heart of the city, I hop off the bus and go into a bakery to get a challah or something like it. I'm told there are several types of braided breads that are not challahs, but I don't know the difference. The cashier asks me something that I don't figure out until later: "Whole grain or white?" The woman next to her asks me if I got it from up front. I did. She tells the cashier which it is, though I don't remember which she said. I'll find out when I make my Shabbat dinner before heading out for another midnight shift.

Saturday, June 2nd, 2018 **4:22 PM**

The billboard just before the coastal road and the Industrial Zone rotates images and videos to entertain and entice us while we're stuck in traffic. Ads for flights to New York, London, and elsewhere flash past, with prices in dollars and Euros, never shekels. Ads for performances by touring stars, several months in advance, pulse in sync with unheard soundtracks. Here, the pop bands are a big thing. Back in the States, they might just be another act at a second-tier venue. Teaser trailers for movies show the names of stars, spelled out in Hebrew. Charlize Theron's name stays onscreen long enough for me to sound it out. I can only decipher the first names of others. It's much harder when the names don't have vowels. Another ad flashes the words "New York, America, Canada," stacked above each other in large print. I don't know the context. Behind and above them, a cut-out figure of a founder of the nation, several stories tall, glares down at us from atop a water tower. The blue sky glows through the holes in the image. We sit in traffic long enough to see small high clouds drift through and past him toward the sea.

Sunday, June 3rd, 2018 **7:36 AM**

In the small park outside the House of a Hundred Grandmothers: men and women sit on or near benches, some in wheelchairs and some not, some with caregivers and some not. In a fenced-in play area, a boy and two girls, one much taller than the others, run in circles around two adults and a jungle gym. They start and stop abruptly. They might be playing something like tag or Mother May I, but from where I am, I can't tell. A deep blue motorcycle sits, as always, just outside the fence. Another one, painted identically, is often there but is gone right now. The bulletin board is empty. I've only ever seen death notices on it, but they last no more than a week. A stream of echoing orchestra music plays faintly from a nearby apartment. As I walk away, it is supplanted by the usual sounds of life on the narrow street: children, birds, and barking dogs. A trumpeter plays a solo from a window at the other end of the block. I hear him start, stop, play a worrying phrase several times, then start again. His sound disappears as I enter a second park on my brief walk home.

Monday, June 4th, 2018 **11:36 AM**

Halfway through the morning, a quartet of starlings screeches and battles in the middle of the street. Sometimes together, sometimes in ever-changing duels, only once in a trio with the other looking on, they peck and tumble, not caring about their surroundings. Curious cats circle at a distance but don't interfere. The birds only scatter when a bicyclist bursts in to their space from around the bend. He slows once past there to slap hands with a man wearing a baby harness. The baby looks around, sagely approving of what he sees. Just past them, a garbage truck backs into the street. A trashman, walking behind it and to one side, directs north and southbound cars, more bicyclists, and me. When he waves in my direction, I step between the truck and a group of now-empty cans and continue on to work.

Tuesday, June 5th, 2018 **8:48 AM**

"The thing with Americans is they always give you a big smile like fake friends then ask you half a question. They want you to feel like a loser when you don't read their mind. It is all power games, like everyone wants to have power over everyone else, like you have to do something to earn their respect. Here, we start with respect. We start even. Believe me, if we want something from you, if we like you, if we don't like you, you'll know it and know what we want. Yes, there are rip-offs in business, in government, in contracts. But person to person, you get the truth, maybe more than you expect."

Tuesday, June 5th, 2018 **11:17 PM**

At the heart of the city, workers from our largest bookstore chain scurry about with tables and boxes. It's Book Week. They're setting up a display that takes up much of the square. The north end has children's and young adult books. Board games are just south of them, followed by general reading and non-fiction. (Later, I look up the word that turns out to mean "non-fiction.") As I sound out the authors' names, I recognize many books as translations of ones that I have known. Once again, I find myself missing my bookselling days. It's after dusk, and they haven't finished setting up yet. I wonder if the display will be open all night. I wonder how they will keep it from being looted or damaged when it is closed. I wonder if that just doesn't happen here. I wonder if I should ask them, but that might seem suspicious and could involve conversations with more Hebrew than I can handle when I'm this tired. I'll be back through here several times in the next few days and nights. I'll see how it goes.

Thursday, June 7th, 2018 **5:27 AM**

Outside the market, where five streets meet, a guitarist is playing and singing through a portable amp. His voice is beautiful. I sit down in a lawn chair in the square and take paper out of my pocket. A notebook lies, apparently abandoned, on a table nearby. Two men, walking a small dog, stop and pick it up. One reads something dramatically in an accent that I can't decipher. They put the notebook down and walk away. When I look up from my writing, the guitarist is gone.

Friday, June 8th, 2018 **6:19 AM**

A Give-and-Take box has sprouted on a sidewalk bench nearby. The last time that I passed it, it held a single children's CD. The time before that, there was also a glass serving plate, still in its open packaging. Another box, near the supermarket, is filled with English-language trade paperbacks of former pulp bestsellers. This one now holds two plastic bags. One is packed with women's garments that I can't identify at a glance, as well as a single shoe. The other holds six translucent iPhone cases, fitting the older, smaller phones that are still more common here. I consider taking one but don't. My current case is secure and sufficiently attractive. Many random objects have traveled here with me for reasons that I can't recall. Some of them might be waiting for their moment in the box, in hopes that they might find a welcoming home.

Saturday, June 9th, 2018 6:17 AM

Rainbow flags fly over the shore road, across from the hotels. The Pride parade is in the city just south of ours, but I can't get there this year. At the heart of my city, it's just another Friday. Buses are crowded with soldiers coming home. Supermarket shoppers collide like overheated particles. Few apologize. The city's small book fair, still up across the street, is less frenzied than the one I visited in the larger city two nights before. Still, there's little I can both understand and afford. I lug my groceries back to the bus stop so I can go home, unpack, and get some sleep.

Sunday, June 10th, 2018 **6:23 AM**

My alarm awakens me late in the afternoon. I dress and walk three blocks north to visit family at the House of a Hundred Grandmothers. We eat a varied meal, supper for them, breakfast for me. Afterward, I read aloud from *Apartment for Rent,* a beloved children's book. They help me with the unfamiliar words: nail, hallway, ceiling; squirrel, rabbit, ant. When night falls, I join them in the prayers for the end of the Sabbath then briefly go back home. Heading out to work again soon after, I call my mother on the phone. We speak of events and people there and here as I walk down pedestrian and vehicular streets, past the spice merchant's closed shop and the open book fair. I arrive at the bus stop just in time and hop aboard to start another week.

Monday, June 11th, 2018 5:27 AM

On a night off, I awaken in the late afternoon and head out to a local hummus joint for something like breakfast. I'm the last customer. As I'm eating outside, a worker piles up all the other chairs. One of my office team, just off the mid-day shift, wanders by with his bicycle and calls out *"B'teyavon,"* Hebrew for *"Bon appetit."* When I'm done, I walk past the book fair and the pizza joint, which are both still open. Not wanting to head back home quite yet, I go for ice cream. I tell the worker there, in Hebrew, that I want a cone of the cappuccino gelato. The worker replies "It's OK. I speak English. What do you want?" I sigh.

Tuesday, June 12th, 2018 6:28 AM

A stack of white dinner plates caps the short pillar at the end of a pedestrian street. A cat, its fur a softer white, sits on top of them. On this adequate throne, it seems to say, humans can worship its glory. In front of the pillar at the far end of the block, empty boots stand at attention, as if waiting for orders from the cat. Between them: fallen flowers, dust on the paving bricks, and small reminders of pets that had come by before. I step around those. Dogs bark, hidden behind tall fences. The cat looks briefly toward the sound. Unimpressed, it continues to sit on its perch, silently surveying its realm.

Wednesday, June 13th, 2018 **5:24 AM**

Rather than scooping up the hummus with the pita that came with it, the man at the table across from mine has torn the bread up in small pieces and tossed them in the bowl. He stabs them with his fork then dredges the hummus with that. Like my falafel, his plate came with what this place calls chips, thick slices of sweet potato, deep-fried. He doesn't touch them. When he leaves, I'm tempted to grab them from his tray and eat them myself, but, as usual, I worry about breaking some societal rule that I haven't learned yet. When I get up, I see that a truck is blocking the sidewalk and the near lane of traffic. Its panel shows day-glo cupcakes and shouts "Happiness – it's us!" The drivers honking at it disagree.

Posters cover a wide column on the square where the roads meet. The outermost, visible layer announces dance parties, piano lessons, a burlesque show that may be a drag show, and an international Unicode hackathon. Hints of other events, sales, and offers peek out from behind it. I can't tell how deep the history goes. Another nearby pillar, carefully maintained, shows a single well-lit poster for municipal events behind clean, clear plastic: film festivals, the Democracy Pavillion, the current Book Week, and the upcoming local New Orleans Jazz Festival. Just past the square's edge, a woman with a rolling suitcase heaves two green trash bags into an open dumpster. Between the first and the second, a screaming cat launches itself from inside, rushes past three other cats sharing an abandoned meal, and disappears under a fence.

Friday, June 15th, 2018 6:11 AM

A sign at the hospital food court divides it into clear zones. Meat restaurants are to the left, dairy to the right. Families sit clustered at tables throughout. I recognize many as religious Muslims and Jews. More women wear a greater variety of head scarves than I have seen anywhere else. Children sit with their families or run around. One little blond girl cries in her grandfather's arms. Another, almost her twin, zooms around on roller skates, crashing into pillars and trash bins. Maybe they figure that if she's hurt, she won't have to go far for treatment. I stop into the strictly kosher McDonald's before I go upstairs for a visit. I'm surprised that this one doesn't have coffee. At a café at the far end of the court, I get a coffee granita. It's the most expensive one I've ever had, but it's the best.

Saturday, June 16th, 2018 5:48 AM

When I enter the hospital room, I immediately recognize the first voice that I hear. That person, though, is an ocean away. Instead, it's a nurse I've never met, with the same southern New Jersey accent, as thick as canned soup. "Hey, Toms River!" She'd been told I'd be visiting. "I'm Englishtown. You know, the flea market?" I know. Listening to her speak, I guess that she's been here for a long time. She may have learned nursing here. The patient I'm visiting and the other's caregiver both speak English, so that's what she speaks to them. But the medical terms, drug names, and the like are all in perfect Hebrew. She seems to have only used the words here. She pronounces even the shared words with Hebrew's guttural consonants and static vowels. She waves as she rolls her cart out the door. "See you again!" Perhaps. But as pleasant as she and the hospital are, I hope I won't have to come here often.

Sunday, June 17th, 2018 **5:24 AM**

At two different places on my walk toward work, I see hedgehogs waddling down the pedestrian streets. Their feet trot as fast as they can but the tiny steps move them slowly along the road. Each freezes in place when it senses that I'm watching. Perhaps it's trying not to be seen. Taking a better look as they hug the edges of shadows, I wonder if they might be young porcupines instead. I don't get close enough to find out.

Monday, June 18th, 2018 **5:33 AM**

The first bird of the morning, on those mornings when I'm at home, starts up between five and five-thirty AM. It doesn't care when the sun is supposed to rise. It's always the same, or at least one of the same species. It's always annoying. It reminds me that I either should be getting up or should be going to bed, except when it reminds me that, serving both day and night shifts, my bodily rhythms are now completely divorced from the rhythms of the sun or of everyday life. Usually I enjoy birdsong. I think Kate Bush has sung along with one of these. But this one doesn't inspire me to sing. It inspires me to wish that I could sleep.

Tuesday, June 19th, 2018 8:44 AM

"I know how it is, your night work. When I moved from Iran to Germany, I worked seven years in a hospital as a caretaker, all nights. When I came here, I worked thirteen years delivering newspapers. At one and a half AM, I would take a bus. At two and a half, I would be at the station. I would put the papers together and fold them and put them in plastic bags, then deliver them until seven, all in the dark. This night work, maybe it is for younger men. Now I sit here or I stand here at the supermarket, in the morning through the evening. But at night, I can go home."

Wednesday, June 20th, 2018 6:06 AM

I walk past a cluster of caregivers at the House of a Hundred Grandmothers. They are sharing an English word. “Vegetable?” one says, then another: “Vegetable?” At lunch, the server announces what soup they have, then asks us how to say it in English. It is, again, “vegetable,” though when she tries it, it sounds more like “basketball.” Another server summons the chef from the kitchen to the table beyond us, where a gaggle of Grandmothers sit in judgment. This might be a chef’s nightmare: a roomful of Jewish mothers second-guessing his cooking. But instead, they are full of praise. The rice and meat dish turned out exceptionally well, almost as well as if each of them had cooked it herself. Heading out from lunch, I forget my shoulder bag. We get a call about it the moment we get upstairs. When I come back to retrieve it, each Grandmother who is still there tells me that

I forgot it and where it is. The only thing to do is to smile at each and say "Thanks."

Thursday, June 21st, 2018 **7:59 AM**

On the Boulevard of the Beautiful People, I walk down the median toward a rectangle of light lying on the path. A large grid of photographs rests on the bricks, a string of tiny white bulbs marking its boundaries. The frames of the prints reflect the light from the streetlamp, giving the display an even glow. A traveling artist has built this temporary gallery. Carefully lettered signs tell his woeful story, but with a hopeful twist: having lost everything, he says, he now wanders the world, capturing beauty wherever he sees it and presenting it to people in the next place he goes. A set of signs at the front of the grid announces his policy: passersby can spot what they like, take what they want, and pay what they can. I'm not moved to take or pay anything, but the image sticks with me as I walk on.

Friday, June 22nd, 2018 **6:52 AM**

A series of hammocks runs down the center of the median on one block of the Boulevard. Low metal fences line each side of their area but not the ends. Young women, casually but fashionably dressed, lie on several of the hammocks, staring into the sky or into their phones. A sleeping baby rests on the belly of one, an open book on another. Farther down, across from an array of late-night coffee shops and eateries, the front of an otherwise unmarked house pulses with strobes of soft pastel colors, so subtle that I wonder at first if I am seeing them. Chiming bells approach me from my left. Watching the lights, I have stepped into the median's bike lane. I hear them, nod in apology, and step back over the line so they can pass.

Saturday, June 23rd, 2018 5:52 AM

From a distance, as I walk along the Boulevard, I hear the moving wind, a low whistling of buildings and trees. The air where I am, though, is still. It remains still as I travel toward the sound. The whistling takes on tonality. As the reverberations lessen, it separates into phrases the length of a human breath. It's from a café nearby, I imagine, or a house with open windows, playing a disc of new age ambiance. I get closer and see a person in front of a pillar of posters, bobbing and moving to the music. Closer still, I see that he is playing a side-blown bamboo flute. Its pale surface contrasts with the dark skin of his face and hands and with his long black hair. To my surprise, the flute is unamplified. Its natural tone carries well through the still air of the night. The small speaker near him plays a steady drone, so quiet that few other than he can hear it.
As I walk past and beyond him, down the

Boulevard toward the national theater, the sound again reverberates and reverts to a general haze, then to the whistling of disembodied wind. But now I have heard the source of the music and seen the person from whom it flows. I can no longer hear it as mere abstraction, forgetting what I know.

Sunday, June 24th, 2018 **6:15 AM**

Children race past me into the elevator at the House of a Hundred Grandmothers. They seem to be playing a game of three-dimensional tag or hide-and-seek. They argue: "There are stairs to the left." "No! He'll expect us. We'll go to the right." They run back out. In the dining hall, Grandmothers summon the kitchen staff again. They don't approve of a set of pastries: someone sprinkled the tops with flour rather than powdered sugar. I think the pastries, round buns with fruit filling, are wonderful as they are, but my taste buds might be too forgiving. When I leave, the lobby's sliding doors don't automatically slide. They are still in Sabbath mode, so they don't sense me approaching. I open them by hand, but I'm too tired to try to explain the problem in Hebrew to the guard. I wave at him and manually work the doors. He nods. I hope he understands.

Monday, June 25th, 2018 8:31 AM

Right before my stop, the local bus makes a detour that I don't expect, into the neighborhood just east of mine. It feels like a different world. My neighborhood has relatively straight streets with large houses and greenery everywhere. Here, dusty roads barely wide enough for the bus twist and loop, packed like intestines into a space that seems too small to hold them. Small houses are crammed next to and behind one another. Worn metal awnings stretch above their doorways, shading the concrete slabs that serve as porches. Looking more closely, though, it's not quite as desolate as it first seemed. The endless houses are punctuated by occasional stores, parks, and community centers. Bright banners and bulletin boards announce and celebrate events. Still, it feels too cramped for me, in its own pocket universe connected by only a few roads and infrequent buses to mine. I almost moved into that neighborhood but I got lucky, finding a much larger apartment with close to the same rent as the ones I'd looked at there. The bus eventually comes back out of the neighborhood at the same point that it went in. I'm glad that I got a better sense of the place, but I'm equally glad that I didn't move there.

Tuesday, June 26th, 2018 **6:05 AM**

My bus crawls along the well-lit street, honking as it goes. We are stuck behind two bicyclists riding next to each other, effectively blocking both lanes. They don't seem to notice us or much else as they meander along, staring into their phones. As we creep forward, a man in a security guard's outfit stands and yells at some people seated behind him, who appear to be ignoring him. I have no idea what he's saying. I do notice that he is making an "sh" sound in words where I would expect an "s." I don't know if this is a speech impediment or part of a dialect that I haven't heard before. Fortunately, at a large intersection, we turn left as the bicyclists go straight and get out of our way. Once past them, though, we get stuck again. The right lane of the road past the mall is only open to buses, but there's no way in. A tractor blocks the entrance. Cones line the inner edge of the lane. Our driver pulls up alongside the cones, stops, and honks again. The man in the tractor gradually looks up, puts down his sandwich, and lopes over to the bus. He and the driver gesture at each other without speaking. He removes some of the cones, and we pull into the bus lanes. Beyond the next stop, workmen under bright lights dig a hole the size and shape of a grave. I hope they are just burying cables.

Wednesday, June 27th, 2018 5:24 AM

According to the solar-powered display, my bus has been due in six to nine minutes for the past twelve. As I wait, I see a young girl with implausibly long hair walking in circles trying to take the perfect selfie. When I catch a glimpse of the image on her phone, I can see that she has settled on just the right camera angle to capture most (but not all) of her face. She is still searching for the perfect background. It's apparently one without me in it. As she stares into the screen, focused on what's behind her, she doesn't see the electric scooter directly in her path. The rider sees her just in time and swerves, almost (but not quite) falling over. I look up and see that my bus is now seventeen minutes away. My house is a ten-minute walk from here, and that last espresso has kicked in. Time to go.

Thursday, June 28th, 2018 **6:05 AM**

A man leaps out from behind a purple curtain on a panel truck and lands in a superhero crouch. Standing, he turns and pulls a flat of apricots from inside. I walk ahead of him into the produce market. Fresh figs and lychee nuts have just come in. Spotting the small pears that I like, I yank a clear plastic bag from a hook on a pillar. The whole hook comes down. "No problem," the shopkeeper says. He bends and picks everything up with one hand while handing me a red bag with the other. "These are better for you. They're smaller." I get the figs and the pears. They don't have other things I had hoped to find. Produce here is seasonal. When it's gone, it's gone. Stepping outside after paying, I pop a whole fig in my mouth. It is sweet, tender, and warm. I pause by a wall, eyes closed, and relish the texture and flavor, then head next door to get my laundry.

Friday, June 29th, 2018 **5:41 AM**

I have walked too many miles for this shawarma. I started at the port, supposedly a hub of urban nightlife. What's there in late evening: closed boutiques, expensive restaurants, and the same chain cafés as my own neighborhood. On the patios, glittering people, mostly speaking English, laugh too loud and nibble at food I don't recognize. I follow the boardwalk around, then walk through an unlabeled park. Close to midnight, children still play on swings and merry-go-rounds. One girl spins quickly on a platform around a pole. Her long hair traces her circuit, flowing parallel to the ground. I find a familiar main street and walk along it. It's much longer than it seems from the bus. On most blocks, nothing is happening. At occasional bars, people stare at projection screens showing the World Cup live. I end up down near City Hall, where I used to catch my bus home after

Hebrew class. Across from it, I stop at a shawarma joint that I've never tried. The food is excellent. Next time, I may start by eating there, then try this journey in reverse.

Saturday, June 30th, 2018 5:30 AM

I sit at a table at the cheap chain cafe at 9 AM, catching my breath between a long night's work and my Friday morning shopping. Children with ice cream cones walk with mothers carrying groceries. Waves of the scent of pot smoke continually drift past me, though I can't tell from where. I get what looks like a different brand of chicken at the grocery store, though it may be the same, only packaged differently. Instead of an onion, I get a beet to roast inside it. As treats, I get an Asian pear and some pomegranate nectar, so rich and sweet that I drink it like wine. The bus comes as I try to decode what's been scrawled on the bus stop. The graffiti will wait. It's time to go home.

Sunday, July 1st, 2018 **6:02 AM**

The moon, nearly full and almost round, rises quickly past the Heart of the City mall. At first I think it's a streetlight behind the trees. It moves higher in the sky, and I see it as it is, shining from beyond low clouds. Its surface with its signature shadows becomes clear as it slides into the empty band of sky above them. It seems to be wobbling slightly, to the left then to the right and back. This must be an illusion, caused by my tired eyes. The moon goes back behind another higher, denser band of clouds. It isn't going to rain. Those clouds are dust from the desert that hovers here, above our heads, in our lungs, and beneath our feet.

Monday, July 2nd, 2018 7:42 AM

The woman tilts back in her chair, closes her eyes, and moves her hands together then apart. “I’ve been here for decades and seen these people come and go. You and I, we came here because we’re committed to the land. But some of these others? They only came here to work. Some work only as hard as they need to, to avoid being sent home, to Moldova, to Ghana, to wherever. I’ve never even heard of some of the places they’re from. Some decide to stay, some because it’s better here, some because it’s so much worse where they’re from, poor places, dangerous places. Many of them put in the hard work, put in the sweat, and earn a way to belong here. It’s hard for them, living here, and they’ll never be like us. We’re here because we believe in being here, returning to our home. There’s a place for them, too, I guess. But not like us.” She opens her eyes and looks at me. I give a noncommittal nod.

The Meatless Market event at the mall is larger than I expected. Several long pop-up tables down the center of a wing carry a wide variety of foods, all of them, I guess, vegetarian. Some of them just have the same fruits and vegetables as the supermarket around the bend, though more are organic and most are overpriced. Some have warming trays of various gops and gloops that I can't identify, ready to be spooned out into to-go containers. My niece is hungry, and this looks better than the food court, so she gets a wrap. I get one too. The woman behind the counter, about my age and with a white head-scarf, warms a thin circle of bread on something like a convex crepe stone. She layers onto it a thin dairy sauce, tabbouleh, chickpeas, olive oil, a sliced egg, and spices. She speaks Hebrew to my niece but hears her speaking English to me. "Where is he visiting from?" My niece answers “He has moved here from the US.” The woman beams. “Welcome!” She hands us our wraps. Walking away, I realize that she has given me back too little change, but I decide not to argue. The wrap is good. My niece teaches me the corresponding Hebrew slang: it is “in the place.” Even at a few shekels over the right price, it’s worth it.

Wednesday, July 4th, 2018 **5:15 AM**

My coffee should be ready in a minute, I've given my name as "Yosef," since baristas can't seem to handle "Joe." The "J" sound is rare in Hebrew, only heard in loan words. The vowel, sliding from "o" to "u," completely throws them. I've seen them write down "Charlie," "Shu," and worse. On the other hand, some of the menu still baffles me. The image of one pastry looks tempting, but I don't know its name. It's written as the word for "baked item" plus the consonants "prg". Is it "parg"? "prag"? "pereg"? As frustrated as I am, I've learned to sympathize with those who struggle with English and its far more cryptic spelling. The barista calls my name as "Yosef" and hands me my cappuccino and the date pastry that I had recognized on the menu. I sit at a table and write while waiting for a friend.

Thursday, July 5th, 2018 6:09 AM

In the lunchroom, the big screen shows the World Cup. Workers stare at it, engrossed and chattering. Onscreen, men run back and forth on grass. Some kick things. Some fall over. I've heard announcers in English, Hebrew, Russian, German, and something I can't make out. They share the same cadences: a steady patter that rises in pitch and tempo as the camera movement gets faster then hits a long high syllable when the people cheer the most and the men on the screen stop running. It's a curious endeavor, somewhat like dance, except that other men decide which groups of running men win and lose, and people who aren't playing are emotionally invested in their doing so. I wander off when I'm done eating. It will still be there when I return. The men onscreen will be doing the same things. Most, I expect, will be wearing different shirts.

Friday, July 6th, 2018 **7:01 AM**

On a night off, I wander downtown to get something to eat. The owner of my favorite local hummus joint sees me coming, waves, and shakes his head. They have already closed. I get a good falafel and some ice cream nearby, then talk to my mother on the phone as I sit outside. On the way home, I get lost twice. I'm used to walking these streets in the dark toward downtown but not back. Streets that I normally walk on autopilot are unfamiliar when taken in reverse. I have walked them so often that I have forgotten their names, so the few signs don't help. I walk straight through turns that I should take, and have to wander back. It's rather like discovering a whole new town, just like mine, but everything's in the wrong order. At least, in this mirror universe, my key still works in the lock when I get home and the water I drink is still cold. And when I see my reflection, the goat-beard that I shaved off months ago is still no longer there.

Saturday, July 7th, 2018 5:32 AM

As I do my Friday shopping, I see containers for coin donations by the registers at most of the stores. They've been there all along, but I hadn't noticed them until someone pointed them out today. The oblong or cardboard cans have coin slots like piggy banks. The charities must be able to open, empty, and reuse them. Many of them are dented. Their peeling paint reveals rust. At the home goods store, cans collect funds for religious charities, medical needs, children with autism, and other causes. At the bakery, produce store, supermarket, and falafel shop, some are the same and some different. I can't identify what most are; the names are obscure or use Hebrew terms that I can't quite make out. As I look at them today, I don't actually see anyone putting anything into them, but they're continually there, totems of community, aid, and religion that have become such an accepted part of the marketplaces that they don't stand out at all.

Sunday, July 8th, 2018 **5:29 AM**

The cab drivers here are good at handling wheelchairs. The city has a large elderly population, so they need to know how to do it. I'm not that skilled, though, at getting someone who uses a wheelchair out of a cab at a curb, especially when we're juggling a portable oxygen unit. Fortunately, the person waiting for the cab we're getting out of works at the House of a Hundred Grandmothers. While I take the wheelchair from the driver, now that he's deftly gotten it from the trunk and put the pieces back together, she handles much of the rest of the process. I get tangled up, though, when trying to back the chair away from the cab. We hit a small stanchion and get stuck. The worker sees this and directs the maneuver so that we can get clear. With a cheerful *"Shabbat shalom,"* she hops into the cab as we head into the mall.

Monday, July 9th, 2018 **5:34 AM**

On my way to work, I see what looks like a person slumped over on the bench with the Give-and-Take box. I walk more quickly toward it, fearing that something has happened to to the man who is often there, smoking and reading late at night. When I get closer, I relax: it's a large duvet that has slid partway to the ground. The box itself is empty. All the books that I had left there last week have been taken, a few at a time. Last night, a collection of children's books and toys and a pink plastic dollhouse were there. They're also gone. A few small white circles, concave and delicate, rest at the bottom of the box, petals that have fallen from the flowers on the trees above the bench. I wonder if I could use the duvet, but decide that I can't, and wouldn't want to drag it to work and back. When I pass the bench the next night, the duvet, too, has disappeared.

Tuesday, July 10th, 2018 **5:16 AM**

All the cats are out tonight. I see three in my yard before I reach the gate, three more on a doorstep on the pedestrian street, and five, joined by a sixth as I watch, nibbling at kibble that someone has carefully strewn on a curb. Several more pass me on their nightly patrols. Two face each other in front of colorful trash cans, howling in rhythmic unison. Many more dogs than usual are out walking with their humans. Everyone but me is wearing shorts and light shirts. I'm wearing khaki pants and long sleeves, since the thermostat in my office is usually set to "Siberia." The tables outside the ice cream shops are busy. I think of stopping at one myself, but I see my bus in the distance. Duty calls.

Wednesday, July 11th, 2018 7:43 AM

I wander into the doctor's waiting room at 8 AM. He and his receptionist are conferring in his office. The door is open. It's a small space. The office itself has a desk, two chairs, and an examining table, without much equipment. The waiting room has another desk and five more chairs. The doctor, originally from South Africa, is quite good. The receptionist, a native here but near-fluent in English, is excellent. To get some prescriptions renewed, I just drop in. She scans my healthcare card, types some things into her computer, then looks into the doctor's office. He says "OK." She sends the prescriptions on to the pharmacy. She notes that I'm due for some tests and hands me completed paperwork and supplies. In moments, I'm headed back down the street to get the prescriptions filled.

Thursday, July 12th, 2018 **8:15 AM**

We've all taken numbers to wait our turn at the pharmacy. We shouldn't have to stand in line, but there's no place to sit down. The numbers advance glacially toward mine. On the TV screens, next to them, news headlines scroll past, but they're too small and moving too quickly for me to read. When my number is called, the pharmacist scans my card. All my medications are in stock. He doesn't need to count out pills. Everything is in cardboard boxes of set numbers of blister packs, kept in a large wall of drawers behind the counter, alphabetized in English. They aren't free, but are relatively cheap. I pile the three-month supplies of everything into a plastic bag and head off to continue shopping.

Friday, July 13th, 2018 **8:27 AM**

"Good morning, John!" The supermarket greeter gives me his usual grin and handshake. For the first couple of months, I had told him each time that my name is actually Joe, but I've given up. "You appear exhausted from your nights of work," he says. Another customer comes up to us. "This man only speaks English? You should speak Hebrew to him." The greeter shrugs. A man with a cane waves his free hand. "Our friend speaks every language, whenever he can." He and the greeter exchange a few sentences of what I think is Turkish. An older woman comes out of the store. "You have no chairs where I can sit down?" The greeter gestures graciously. "For you, of course!" He takes a price sign off a stack of white plastic chairs, then lifts the top few off and puts one from the middle on the ground. "Here, for you, a beautiful clean one that won't get your white skirt dirty."

The woman nods and sits down. More people come by. They speak even more languages. I go in to finish my shopping so I can get home and finally go to sleep.

Saturday, July 14th, 2018 — 5:25 AM

I fall asleep at my desk while writing. Rather than the usual sounds and images, I dream in this narrative voice. Waking up, I am surprised by how much I remember: "The girl on the unicycle sings her viola as she weaves between graffiti. The cats are Asimov. Two are a duvet. The fourth eats a bus stop that I can't understand. In the passage, a truck is improvising. 'Coffee,' she says, 'makes your shirts too tall.'" I jot this in my notebook, then go to the bathroom and to bed.

Sunday, July 15th, 2018 **10:19 AM**

"I saw her at lunch today, in the dining hall at the House of a Hundred Grandmothers. She sat there quietly, staring at her soup. She took a few sips of water. She's had a fascinating life. She's a friend of mine. You see that, up on my shelf? She made that herself, by hand. And now? At lunch she wouldn't eat. The soup, the main course, the salad, anything. Finally she took some ice cream with her back to her room. Maybe she'll eat it there."

Monday, July 16th, 2018 5:30 AM

The couple getting on the bus are squabbling in something that sounds like French but isn't. The phonemes are the same, but they're in the wrong order. Their children are grabbing at the plush toys on the dashboard. I recognize Taz, Daffy Duck, a heart, and Minnie Mouse. Other toys are too abstract or too worn to identify. Garlands of flowers dangle from the rear-view mirror. Decals near the door say "Trust in God" and "Smile, it's all good." The driver lets the bus swerve as he tries to grab back the toys. He clearly trusts in God. But he doesn't smile.

Tuesday, July 17th, 2018 9:48 AM

I don't know how far away the ambulance is or where it's coming from. The hard glass storefront windows on the busy street reflect all light and sound. I back away from the curb to stay clear of whatever's coming. An electric scooter zooming up the sidewalk almost hits me from behind. Ignoring the signals, the rider crosses the street in the middle of the block. The ambulance, coming around the corner, has to dart around him. The scooter rider gestures and yells. Clearly, the ambulance's business was less important that what had absorbed his attention on his earbuds and his phone.

Wednesday, July 18th, 2018 5:29 AM

A poster at the bus stop, echoed all over the city, shows a woman with perfect hair placing her finger to her lips. From the minimal Hebrew text, I guess that it advertises an album, "My Secret," by an artist I don't know, Eve Rosheh. Looking more closely, I see the image of a small round container at the bottom of the ad, with English writing on it. Apparently, the name is Yves Rocher (isn't Yves a man's name?), and it has something to do with cosmetics. Given that information, I now know less about the product than I thought I knew before.

Thursday, July 19th, 2018 — 7:10 AM

The silence on the bus is pierced by bursts of feedback as the driver fiddles with a microphone. He may be trying to tell us something. After a few blasts, he gives up. It may have to do with the twin girls who are climbing over the seats in front of me as if they were at a playground. I glance at their grandmother and raise an eyebrow. She gestures at them, “What can we do?”, and sighs. The twin in the unicorn party hat looks at me and whispers in her sister’s ear. They giggle then dive down behind the seats and disappear.

Friday, July 20th, 2018 **5:38 AM**

They're trying out a new voice for the announcements on the bus. It's gentler, slower, with a wider dynamic range – and almost inaudible over air conditioning, conversation, or traffic. Only the upper frequencies of the consonants come through. The original voice still says "The next stop is:", but it's followed by clicks and murmurs. Three of the key bus stops are at malls. The one at which I get off for work sounds like a "k" followed by a brief mumble. The one at which I change buses to go home mumbles for a while longer. And the big one along the way, which is never open when I pass it going to or from the night shift, has a few more consonants mixed in. I can rarely tell what It's saying for other stops, and the onboard signs are even less dependable. I actually have to look outside to see where I am.

Saturday, July 21st, 2018 **9:45 AM**

Almost all of the writing on the t-shirts here is in English. The only Hebrew is on a few teenagers' identical shirts. Each shows a white shield on a deep blue background, but all of these teens wear backpacks obscuring the text. Many of the English shirts are for rock bands. I see Judas Priest, AC-DC, Jethro Tull, and lots of Metallica. Several kids wear iconic Joey Ramone shirts. Few had been born when he died. Many women's shirts shout slogans in bold block print. "Start Your Revolution" walks past "Dance Dance Dance" and "Most Quiet Weed." Two men wearing "Not Your Toy" and "Stupid Boy" walk hand in hand. I can't figure out what one woman's shirt is trying to say. I get closer and see that the shirt is splattered with arbitrary streams of letters, a bit like Cage's "Mesostics re: Merce Cunningham", though I doubt the designer had heard of that. Still, there may be a hidden message. As in Hebrew, I just have to throw the right vowels at it. It may eventually make sense.

Sunday, July 22nd, 2018 5:23 AM

On the night of the fast of the Ninth of Av, I gather with other men near the entrance to the synagogue at the House of a Hundred Grandmothers. They have recruited me to help form the group of ten worshipers that they need for a community reading of the Book of Lamentations. As we wait, flashing red lights come into the parking lot. Their reflections zoom around the lobby. Four people in uniforms enter. "Where is the sick person?" No one knows. They give a room number. It's in Acute Care. "Oh, yes, it must be the Romanian woman." They wheel a fully loaded gurney down the hall and around a corner. After several phone calls, the group gives up on finding ten men. Perhaps they will in the morning. I head out, ducking around the ambulance in the driveway and past scattered people sitting on park benches in the dark.

Monday, July 23rd, 2018 12:16 PM

The dumpster is covered with books: atlases, histories, novels in several languages, and various sacred texts. Traditionally, we don't discard those texts, but the people throwing them out might not know that. Digging through the stacks, I uncover the slot on the dumpster's lid and look inside. It's completely filled with books, plus a few DVDs and magazines. I suspect that someone might be clearing out a relative's apartment, not caring what they find or not having the time to select and save things. I take a few books, including the sacred texts: volumes of prayers and psalms, apparently editions for soldiers, with surprisingly beautiful designs, plus an amazing reproduction of a fifteenth century illustrated bible. I wish I could bring all the remaining books to a Give-and-Take box or to a bus or train station's bookshelves, but I don't have a way to transport them. Perhaps magical book fairies will spirit them away during the night.

Tuesday, July 24th, 2018 **5:24 AM**

A mound of red dirt, several stories tall, is rising at the center of town. It's as if archaeologists, rather than digging through an ancient tel, were constructing a new one, so people millennia from now could learn about us from the junk we left behind. They're going to be building apartments there, hundreds of them in one city block. Our central bus station used to be there. I'd been to it long ago, but only vaguely remember it. Buses still stop on the streets around the fenced-in space. A new bus station is about to open a few kilometers away, out near the train station, along a street with shaggy topiaries on its median strip. I don't think it will have a building at all. And two new train stations have opened in the next town. One is closer to my house than my own town's station. Some day when it's light out and I'm awake, I'll have to wander over there and check it out.

Wednesday, July 25th, 2018 5:21 AM

On my doorstep, a cockroach stalks a much smaller lizard. When they see each other, each freezes in place, as does the kitten watching from above. I don't think any of them wants to eat any of the others, but they remain wary. They don't seem to notice the giant figure moving above and around them as I step out the door.

Thursday, July 26th, 2018 **5:28 AM**

I walk down the dark path to my gate. I stop when I look across the road. Someone matching my size and build is silhouetted on the opposite path, also standing still. My first thought is that I'm looking in a mirror, but I quickly remember that there has never been a mirror there nor any reason for one. After a moment, the light behind it, perhaps a motion sensor, clicks off. When it clicks on again, the figure is gone. A battalion of cats bursts through the open gateway and scatters. One, black with a white spot on its head, runs up to me, rubs its head against my foot, then disappears into the darkness.

Friday, July 27th, 2018 **5:19 AM**

The bus may have skipped the train station. Or maybe I just didn't notice it. There's a lot of noise going on at once: the radio blaring some sort of argument, the driver talking on his phone, the stop announcements, two groups of teenagers having unrelated conversations, and various flashing marquees and billboards outside. It never quite turns into simple static. Instead, streams of words and images, remaining distinct, compete for attention. Words in Hebrew mostly shoot past, but the frequent bits of English in the signs and voices jump out as if illuminated. I'm not headed to the train station, and it doesn't really matter to me if we were there or not. But not having seen it is an even more disorienting surprise.

Saturday, July 28th, 2018 **12:20 PM**

"He's been here for a while. (Yes, there are grandfathers at the House of a Hundred Grandmothers.) He's a widower. When he came here, his father was still alive, living here too. He was a technician, then his job ended, and he had some health problems and a stroke. He speaks slowly now, and can be hard to understand. But he's always learning. Every day, he's up in his room, taking courses at the open university. He's good to talk to, though he doesn't seem to understand that women can be educated, too. He always asks my husband questions. But I have my own college degrees too, you know."

Sunday, July 29th, 2018 3:33 PM

The new cheesemonger wears an unlabeled baseball cap and a Gravity Crash t-shirt. He's fairly young, but is already missing many of his teeth. I ask him for the least expensive cheese that I see in the deli case, a tenth or less of the price of what surrounds it. He doesn't recognize the name and comes around front to look. I point. He nods and retrieves the block of cheese from the case. The woman next to me looks up. "Have you tried it? How do you use it?" In omelettes, I tell her, and in sandwiches. The cheesemonger starts to slice the cheese then stops. "I can make it thinner, OK?" I nod. He turns a dial on the slicer, puts the cheese that's already been through it in and runs it again, then removes the cheese and packages it. "And for you, ma'am?" he asks the other customer. "I'll have the same thing," she says. "Really? Would you like to taste it first?" She shakes her head. "If he likes it, I'll try it." Not everyone likes the cheap cheese. I hope it works well for her.

Monday, July 30th, 2018 5:33 AM

On hot nights, when I pass his throne room, the man is always there. He sits on a plastic chair, perfectly centered in the space. A few square meters of scrappy lawn surrounds him. Grass doesn't grow well here. But the bushes on three sides are lush and beautiful. Yellow flowers bloom on those to his left, purple flowers to his right. Tree branches, hanging over and into the square, form a canopy with more flowers, some red and some white with pink near the stem. More flowers grow where the bushes meet the ground. He sits there silently, without a shirt. His khaki skin matches his shorts and sandals. His grey hair and mustache and his blue eyes contrast with them and complement the flowers. We rarely speak, other than a brief "Good evening," "A peaceful Sabbath," or "Good day." But I know he sees me pass, as he sees the cats, birds, and hedgehogs. I'm part of the ecology now.

Tuesday, July 31st, 2018 **5:52 AM**

The woman at the bus stop has simple questions for me, but I can't answer her. I understand her, but when I try to respond, I can't recall some Hebrew words that I need: Sign. Direction. Arrive. She rolls her eyes and walks away. The next person to approach me waves a lighter in the air and speaks in rapid-fire Russian. I have no idea what he's saying. Seeing this, he switches to broken English. He's supposedly selling his father's beloved heirloom Zippo lighter for fifty shekels so he can get something to eat. I decline. He stomps off. I look up at the electronic sign and see that my bus, which had been due in a moment, has now decided not to show up at all. The next one is in twenty minutes. I mutter in frustration. At least when I talk to myself, I usually understand what's being said.

Wednesday, August 1st, 2018 5:31 AM

From the way this guy is standing at the falafel joint, I can tell he's an American. He's leaning on the counter, his elbow jutting across it as if he owns everything, studiously looking away while glaring side-eye at the workers. They and the other customers have seen these aggressively casual antics before. When he finally takes his elbow down and stands like everyone else, they stop ignoring him. He says simply "Falafel." From his accent, I know I was right. The worker asks him in detail what he'd like on it. He clearly doesn't understand what's being said but tries to hide it by acting like he doesn't care. He pays with a large bill, again leaning on the register and waving it as he looks in another direction to show off how little money means to him. The worker takes it and puts too little change down on the counter. It takes the guy a moment to see the change. He scoops it up and stuffs it in his pocket. He appears not to realize that he's been stiffed. Everyone else does. Nobody says a thing.

Thursday, August 2nd, 2018 **5:29 AM**

An array of salads and other fixings fills the customers' side of the falafel joint's counter. People pile these into their pitas, adding them to what the workers put in. A man my age or older stands there with a half-order, the cheapest thing on the menu. He is wearing an aged, bulging backpack. His sandals are about to fall apart. He may or may not be intentionally growing a beard. He keeps adding the fixings to his half-pita. Each time, he eats what he's put in, carefully not eating any of the pita itself, then adds more. He's blocking the line, but everyone moves around him. This may be all that he's eating today. The workers and customers understand and let him do what's needed to survive.

Friday, August 3rd, 2018 **5:27 AM**

There's a traffic jam of baby carriages on this bakery patio. The one from our extended family, with a baby born a few days ago, is blocking the one with the two-month-old. People stand and shuffle carriages and chairs. The mothers coo at each other's infants. More small children sit with families or wander about. One little girl toddles up to a docile dog and babbles at it in a private language that it seems to understand. Another child sits on the narrow ramp at the exit. She has to get up to allow our party's carriage and wheelchair to leave. Once we've passed, she sits down as she was, her back against the wooden wall, playing with her phone.

Saturday, August 4th, 2018 8:21 AM

The man's grey ponytail flaps in the air as he jumps to reach the roll of plastic bags. I am, as usual, the tallest person in the aisle, so I step over to help. The roll is packed too tightly into the dispenser. I have to turn it a few degrees at a time to release a bag. I pull the bag down, tear it off, and hand it to him. "Thank you," he says, then sighs. "I really need four." No problem. I reach up and gradually pull more out. "Look at this," he says. "You see those dispensers over there? All empty. And the one we can't reach is stuffed full. I spoke to the manager yesterday and he said he'd fix it, but today? Nothing. Things shouldn't be like this. I ask you: We're the Jewish people. We're supposed to be a light to all the nations – and we can't even get this right?"

Sunday, August 5th, 2018 9:34 AM

The streets downtown are quiet, even for a Sabbath afternoon. It's hot, but not as hot as it usually gets in August: we're in the high eighties Fahrenheit, the low thirties Celsius. My taxi rolls past sights I hadn't noticed before: election posters, a For Rent sign atop a mixed-use building, a red banner as wide as the street announcing the entrance to a kibbutz. A topiary at a traffic circle, previously cryptic, has been trimmed to reveal a symmetrical pair of swans. The mayor, up for re-election, has focused on making the city beautiful. Many wish that he would put more energy and funds into needed infrastructure. More people are outside at the beach: women in shorts and sundresses, men with or without shirts, and religious families with long sleeves and skirts designed to cover them yet keep them cool. I arrive at work and head down to my basement office. Deep inside, we can no longer tell the weather, the time of day, or, except for the consistent gravity, exactly which planet we're on.

Monday, August 6th, 2018 **3:01 AM**

"The thing with you Americans is that you can be the shyest person, not wanting to talk to people in real life. But when you have to give a presentation at work or at school, you rock it. You're always nervous, always wondering if you know enough, if anyone will believe you. But you've all been up there your whole life, giving presentations in schools since you were little. You're scared until the lights come on. Then you're onstage. Then you're at home."

Tuesday, August 7th, 2018 **10:58 AM**

The famous clocktower is not where I expect it to be. Making my way down the coast from the newer city to the old, I set my sights on an ancient steeple, far taller than everything else. When I finally get there, after too much time wandering in narrow streets, I find that it's the minaret of a mosque at the edge of the sea. I had walked past the actual clocktower, several blocks away. The real thing is only a few stories tall and scarcely more than a century old. It's quite beautiful, with deep blue stained-glass windows and an exterior that shines like gold in the glow of the hidden lights. Designs that look like careful graffiti on a wooden door are really made of bent strips of metal. I sit and watch it quietly. Its look changes as the sun sets. Endless tourists, not noticing, take selfies there against the door, adding it to their online galleries of places they can show that they have visited. Perhaps, when the images completely circle the globe, they can claim some sort of prize.

Wednesday, August 8th, 2018 2:27 AM

On the square around the clocktower, the new is layered on the old. Strings of electric lights run along the fronts of the buildings that face the tower. Chain clothing stores and currency exchanges are nestled next to small eateries catering to tourists' tastes. I see the first American-style fried chicken place that I've noticed since moving here. I'm tempted to try it, but I go for the hummus joint next door. The workers speak English to everybody, even the group of women speaking German to one another. As I sit and wait for my order, I see how the building has been changed for modern times. What must have been a single long room is now subdivided. Recent plaster fills the space under older arches made of stones and mortar. The long slabs, flat and pale, echo the bits of lamb that spin silently on the vertical shawarma spit below the apex of the arch. Beige meets beige, though in my mind as I picture it later, gold reflects gold.

Thursday, August 9th, 2018 **5:26 AM**

Along the shore, beneath the minaret, clusters of people watch the sun set over the sea. A small group in identical aprons sit together on steps and benches. I imagine that they are temporary staff, hired for a celebration. Two little girls in full wedding dresses, perhaps flower bearers, walk with their mother, who is wearing a tan jacket and shorts. Couples of women, men, and both hold hands and lean into each other. Nuns in what look like light summer habits murmur in French as I stand nearby. As the sun touches the water, even the cats come out and watch, perhaps purring a feline prayer to welcome the night.

Friday, August 10th, 2018 **5:37 AM**

"She was a charming girl, part Scandinavian, part Israeli. She wore these false eyelashes, dark, huge, so heavy she could barely keep her eyes open. She was always fluttering her eyelids, like she was trying not to fall asleep. Nice girl. But she didn't last long here, at the hotel."

Saturday, August 11th, 2018 **5:30 AM**

The barista knows what I'm getting. As I dig a five-shekel coin out of my wallet and approach the counter, she waves a regular-size cold cup and points to the coffee granita machine. Yep. Outside, another barista appears to be doing a complicated dance. As I get closer and overhear the conversation, I see that he's describing a soccer match and replicating some fancy footwork that happened in it. Leaving the shop, I walk through a flock of pigeons. One of them, startled, flies up and collides with a man walking toward us. The man apologizes. The bird doesn't.

Sunday, August 12th, 2018 **10:05 AM**

Sweeping the floor, my broom lifts up the large cockroach that has been lying there on its back. When I first saw it, a couple of days ago, it had been waving its legs about, but I couldn't flip it upright. Now it lies still. I sweep it up, its legs tangled with the broom head. I shake it off just above the floor. It lands on its back again, but, to my surprise, its legs start moving. I brush it gently onto the dustpan, take it outside, and slide it onto the pavement. It lands on its feet. At first slowly, then at its usual speed (they're too big to be fast), it heads into the tall grass. I watch it as it disappears. Another life saved. It's a good day.

Monday, August 13th, 2018 **7:55 AM**

The chess computer is sitting on top of a trash can, the same one on which I found all those books. The machine's a classic, some thirty years old. The case says that it was endorsed by that era's world chess champion. All the pieces are intact. It doesn't power up, but the batteries are probably long dead. Someone who wasn't using it put it out there as a donation to someone who might. I know just the person. I leave behind the stack of Disney videotapes that sit next to it and, tucking the computer under my arm, continue up the hill.

Tuesday, August 14th, 2018 5:12 AM

The House of a Hundred Grandmothers now has a hundred and one. My family's first grandchild has been born. My mother and brother arrive from America to celebrate. Some of us meet each other for the first time, some for the first time in decades. My siblings and I can't quite pin down the last time we all were together, but it was before the new mother herself was born. We gather for lunch and for pictures. Great-grandmother, grandmother, mother, and newborn daughter pose for a photo together. Other, unofficial grandmothers drift by. They give their blessings to the four generations gathered at last.

Wednesday, August 15th, 2018 **10:17 AM**

The older city looks different, now that I know the way out. Scouting the destination for a future trip, I find that I've entered the city again. I follow the map carefully, trusting it even where it's counter-intuitive. I come around a corner and see the minaret, silhouetted by a neon-red sun beneath the sliver of a crescent of the nearly new moon. The call to prayer, sounding the same as the last time I'd been there, echoes about. It's odd in its lack of oddness: the steady rhythm of the unaccompanied voice, the tonality, and what seem like implicit key changes sound western, without the bent notes and ornaments that I'd come to expect. As it fades, I wonder if I'd really been hearing something else.

Thursday, August 16th, 2018 6:32 AM

As I walk through the hotel, past the lobby and up to my family's rooms, I recognize how my current job has changed what I see. Before, the guests stood out. I was vaguely aware of the people who worked there, seemingly transient, translucent. Now, I am acutely aware of the workers who surround us: the valet, the porter, the manager and staff at the front desk, the waiters, the cleaners, and the people doing repairs. Guests drift by like ghosts, getting less of my attention. It's the same as how my mind's eye sees lines of code and the people writing them when I use computers, lighting and lenses and people at editing desks when I watch video, and workers shelving and removing product and helping customers in retail stores. Once the curtain is lifted and we see the gears and people behind the scenes, the surfaces of the commonplace can never look the same again.

Friday, August 17th, 2018 **6:56 AM**

Putting the baby to bed in her stroller is complex and hazardous. The grandfather, standing, gradually moves her up and out, away from his shoulder. I take the blanket that her head had rested on. The grandfather, supporting her head, tilts her so that she is facing upward. He rotates her so that she is facing in the opposite direction and lowers her. The mother, seated, moves her hands upward and under his. He slides his hands away so that the baby is now in her arms. She rotates, pulls the baby inward toward her then away, and positions her above the stroller, parallel to it. I place the blanket in the stroller, smoothing it against the surface and the sides. The mother lowers the baby into the stroller, moving more slowly as she gets closer. Her arms make contact with the surface. She slides her arms from under the baby. Her right hand slides out, almost imperceptibly, from under the baby's head, until the baby lies on her own in the stroller. She remains asleep. The maneuver is a success. The eaglet has landed.

Saturday, August 18th, 2018 **5:38 AM**

The tour guide really knows this town. His ancestors founded the neighborhood that we're exploring. It was the first built beyond the walls of the older city, planting the seeds of the new. Here, in this house, his family rejected a suitor who then won a Nobel Prize for his novel of lost love. Over there, a rival got an election overturned and stole the leadership of the city from someone far up the guide's family tree. After the tour, I lead my family through the sensory overload of a huge outdoor bazaar. When we emerge, we catch a bus back to our city and sit in an empty, cool ice cream shop, enjoying the silence.

Sunday, August 19th, 2018 5:37 AM

Younger members of the family come to my place for a light supper before the flight. It's the first time that any of them have been there. My apartment is not as neat as it might be, but it's as neat as it gets. Supper is haphazard; I had only been able to shop for groceries in the moment between yesterday's tour and the closing of the stores for the Sabbath. But they are content, nibbling at pita and dips, playing with a niece's dog, and making video calls back home. We go back to join the rest of the family at the House of a Hundred Grandmothers. We all promise to stay in closer touch, now that we've found the reasons and technologies to do so. After several cycles of hugs, they return to America. I return to work.

Monday, August 20th, 2018 **5:24 AM**

"I know we have a shredder, but I like tearing these papers up by hand. It's therapeutic. I learned it in the army. At the end of every day, we had to tear all the papers into little pieces. I do it now, and I know for sure my shift is done."

Tuesday, August 21st, 2018 11:47 AM

The new train station looks just like all the other ones, designed for efficiency rather than beauty. I pass through an enclosed walkway from the entrance and ticketing area, over a major highway, and down the stairs and elevators to the single platform. One whimsical touch stands out in the passage: the windows bear translucent cartoon-like drawings related to the trains. The images stretch across the corridor in the late afternoon sun. The colors illuminate and transform the white sneakers of a man with a guitar as he walks by.

Wednesday, August 22nd, 2018 **5:31 AM**

Two little girls run past me at the old train station near the beach. As they disappear around a corner, one drops a plastic purse at my feet. I stop and stand there until I see the man who had been calling to them earlier come into view. I wave to him and gesture at the purse. He nods and says "Thank you" in a North American accent as he picks it up and trots after them. I see them a few more times later on, in different tourist-friendly parts of the city. We don't say anything more to each other, but the girl with the purse smiles at me each time.

Thursday, August 23rd, 2018 **5:23 AM**

The buildings on this square are older than most I have seen. Elsewhere, everything looks blunt, oblong, modern. Here, the architecture flows to fit the roads. A curved face and rounded windows front a flat-iron hotel at the acute angle between two streets. Down the block, roofs and porches have crenelations and details designed to be enjoyed. There is some graffiti, but not much. An apparent consensus has determined which surfaces may be decorated and which must be left alone. One wall shows figures of people, cryptic inscriptions, half of a Spider-Man, and, above it all, a clearly written "ouch". Another building that, in another country, I would be sure had been a synagogue, has layers of color near the ground. But the curved carved columns and stained-glass Jewish stars above it are undisturbed.

Friday, August 24th, 2018 **10:16 AM**

There's some graffiti in my city, but not as much as I've seen elsewhere. Most of the art is in a standard international style: large colorful block letters of versions of English words with black or white outlines around them. But some markings around the city seem scrawled by a single person, with a consistent message: There were fourteen commandments, not ten. These hold the key to understanding, to peace, even to war against something (what that might be has been rubbed out). All these proclamations are written in black marker, most on posters or glass, though some mar white stone walls. I try to research what the fourteen might be and why this person might find it so important. I find links and theories online, but they blur into the usual mass of disagreement. I keep an eye out for further writings on the walls.

Saturday, August 25th, 2018 **4:40 AM**

A memorial at the site of the assassination shows once-flat stones in upheaval. The guide says that this shows the way that society was shattered by the event. One wall has graffiti from the aftermath. More walls once did. The guide says that they had meant to preserve the markings, but the art was painted over by mistake. As I look more closely, I see that one word looms above the rest: “We’re sorry.” The square is now named for the fallen leader, so that people remember him when saying the name.

Sunday, August 26th, 2018 5:21 AM

I haven't been on this cobblestone street by daylight. More vehicles may drive on it then. Now, late at night, cars are parked in the crevices of buildings. As I sit here, only two have come by. Each creeps down the middle of the roadway, one headed to my left, one to my right, patiently waiting for the people walking in front of them. Scooters and bicycles, pedaled and electric, roll by. The smaller they are, the more wildly they drive. The animals also follow this law. The largest dogs lumber grandly across the stones, while the roundest cats rarely move at all. The smaller ones run by, spar with one another, and dart into shadows. A cockroach or something like it, several centimeters long, walks toward me evenly, regally, along the ridges of the bench. Smaller than the smallest of the cats, it seems comfortable knowing that it's still the biggest bug around.

Monday, August 27th, 2018 5:25 AM

I should know better than to shop for groceries on a Sunday morning. The stores are closed on Friday nights and Saturdays for the Sabbath, so they haven't restocked. Empty refrigerated bays, like rectangular tundras, lie barren, awaiting produce and meat. Young men guide massive floor-washing machines through the wider aisles. In a narrow aisle, a mother pushes a stroller swiftly, like a battering ram. The child inside laughs whenever it hits a person or display. The mother, focused on the sound coming through her earbuds, doesn't seem to notice. I get most of what I want. I'll have to come back for the rest.

Tuesday, August 28th, 2018 **5:30 AM**

At noon, the cobblestone street has blossomed with the beauty and noise of a twice-weekly arts fair. Tables and booths house kabbalistic astrologers, sellers of crystals for decoration and divination, creators of all kinds of home-made art, and makers of flavored honey. Old men on high tables get massages and healing treatments. In the distance, an electric piano plays "Bohemian Rhapsody," its tinkling timbre reining in the bombast. The neighborhood cats sit out of sight or at the fair's edges, waiting for night to return.

Wednesday, August 29th, 2018 5:29 AM

"I was born here, but my parents weren't. I grew up speaking English at home. When I got to school, they heard me speaking it OK, so they skipped me past some of the learning. So I don't really know how English officially works. I still can't tell what a noun or a verb is. I started speaking Hebrew in school. So it's like I don't have a first language. I have two second languages. And I have to think really hard when I switch from one to the other."

Thursday, August 30th, 2018 **8:32 AM**

As I walk along the darkened path to my front gate, my foot hits something soft and heavy. I nudge it and it moves, bumping into the other foot. I hear a complaining meow. I move forward carefully. It moves with me, tracing an infinity symbol around my ankles. "Keep that up," I growl, "and I'll either place-kick you or trip over you." The cat doesn't speak English. I reach the front gate and open it. The cat doesn't move. I step over it and head out, leaving it to either guard against or protect those who walk on its land. As a mere human, I can't figure out which it means to do.

Friday, August 31st, 2018 **10:09 AM**

"Falafel? On a baguette?!" The teenager looks at his mother in horror. The worker nods to the mother. "Of course we can do that. What, since your son started studying at Technion, he thinks he knows everything that can exist?" The little boy with them snickers. "Since before Technion," he says. The teenager swats him with his open hand. "But falafel on a baguette?" the teenager whines. The worker stares him down. "We have pita. We have baguettes. We have laffa bread. And we have falafel, shawarma, sabich, and even burgers. Anything with anything is possible." I think of flashing a Vulcan salute at him and intoning "Infinite Diversity in Infinite Combinations." But he would probably think I was doing a priestly blessing out of context and would be even more confused.

Saturday, September 1st, 2018 5:28 AM

With time to kill on a hot Friday afternoon, I hop off the bus at the mall to sit for a while in the air conditioning. The food court is busy but some tables are free. The McDonald's is out of frozen drinks. They have already started shutting parts of the kitchen down. I get an iced coffee and sit at a table to write. At precisely 4 PM, metal barriers descend in front of most of the eateries. I see that all the shops within view have closed. The Sabbath is coming. Time to go.

Sunday, September 2nd, 2018 8:01 AM

In the supermarket, a young mother with a stroller juggles three large, light bags of table snacks. Giving up on handling everything, she tilts the stroller back and layers the bags on top of the child. The child throws them off. I scoop them up and hand them back to the mother. She puts them on top of the child again. The child throws them off again, laughing. He thinks it's a game. She doesn't. At the register, my purchases come to more than a hundred shekels, so the cashier offers me a package with a kiddush cup and other items for ten shekels more. I don't go for it, but once I leave the store I wish that I had. I think of asking the multilingual greeter if there's a German word for "reverse buyer's remorse."

Monday, September 3rd, 2018 5:45 AM

The grand opening of the shop on the city square, between the spice merchant and the hummus joint, is mobbed. Flocks of women with plastic glasses of white wine stand around empty card tables. The storefront may be some sort of beauty parlor. There's no sign. The inside, though brightly lit, is so empty that it's hard to tell. Portishead plays from portable speakers. The music clashes with the sound of the accordionist who stands at the far end of the square, playing indistinguishable klezmer tunes and light classics. I get my usual hummus plate and sit down outside, but the stench of cigarettes from the crowd drives me indoors. I look out the doorway as I eat, taking in the sights and sounds, but not the scents.

Tuesday, September 4th, 2018 **10:00 AM**

"She had a hard life at home, back on her island. She couldn't break up her family, but couldn't stay. She left her children with their grandparents and found work and refuge here, caring for us at the House of a Hundred Grandmothers. Someday, she'll go back again. She wants to build herself a new home. And she says that when she does, there will be a big Star of David in the front window, just like our flag, to remind her of the love and comfort she has found here."

Wednesday, September 5th, 2018 11:42 AM

In the Democracy Pavilion, I watch a multimedia presentation in English, alone. A worker comes in partway through. She asks if she might stop and restart the show. A large group of touring nurses has suddenly shown up and wants to see it. It's blisteringly hot outside where they would have to wait. I immediately agree that they should come in. I'm in no hurry. They enter, and their leaders thank me so much that I'm embarrassed. The worker starts the program again, this time in Hebrew. It's well made, showing the divisions and stresses within Israeli society throughout the nation's brief history, without sugar-coating. The nurses thank me again when they leave. The worker asks me if I'd like to see it from the start again, in English. I do. There's so much information in it that once isn't enough.

Thursday, September 6th, 2018 5:34 AM

I try to drink my coffee granita at precisely the right speed: quickly enough to be finished before my bus comes, but slowly enough to avoid a brain freeze. Across the road, another street fair is starting up. Workers test the speakers with Israeli rap. The usual face-painters, dancers, and stilt-walkers are in place. A woman strolls past me in a white gown, with a headdress that looks like rams' horns. (Rosh Hashanah is coming.) I would stay and watch, but I have large bags of laundry and of perishable groceries to bring home, and I need to sleep before my midnight shift tonight. I'll have to catch the next fair. I doubt that they'll have one for Yom Kippur, but they probably will, a few weeks from now, for Sukkot.

Friday, September 7th, 2018 5:29 AM

In the shadow of the clocktower, a small car sideswipes a garbage truck and gets wedged beneath it. No one is hurt, but neither vehicle can move. The cars stuck behind them try to blast them apart with the power of their horns. That only worked for Joshua. I watch from the American-style fried chicken joint on the square as police, emergency workers, the drivers, passersby, tourists, and the valets from the nearby hotel gather and argue. Two women in white headscarves position themselves precisely in front of the scene, turn their backs to it, and take a perfect selfie.

Saturday, September 8th, 2018 4:23 AM

My white baseball cap is now scruffy and stained. Walking to work late at night, I think about whether and how I should clean it. As usual, I flip through the Give-and-Take box on the way. I find a pristine new hat in there, white with the bright blue logo of the city's celebration of Jerusalem Day. I stuff it in my pocket. although I don't know if or when I will need it. As I wait for the bus home in the morning, I feel the first drops of rain since spring. (Rosh Hashanah is coming, and with it the autumn rains.) I pull the hat from my pocket and put it on, just in time.

Sunday, September 9th, 2018 9:33 AM

"Back in the States, I was like eight, nine years old, '93, '94, something like that. So my grandfather asks me to hook up something to his computer to work like a shabbos clock, you know, turn lights on and off at the right times. We had this little rickety box I hooked up to the MIDI port on the PC and to the power line, and it worked. Slow, but it worked. Soon, friends call friends, and I've got a good business going. My grandfather had the electrician's license, so I went in officially under him, just this kid, on my own, and made good money. Not like here – here every single person's gotta have specific papers for everything. It'd never happen now."

Monday, September 10th, 2018 9:05 AM

I get lost trying to find the Acute Care center at the House of a Hundred Grandmothers. It now has a new metal door. A nurse sees me circling around and points me in the right direction. Once again, they have invited me to sing the blessing over wine for the holiday. (Rosh Hashanah is here.) As I enter, people at the tables shush each other and call out "The rabbi is arriving!" I'm not a rabbi, but I'm pleased that they remember me. The melody for the blessing is the same as for Passover, but the words differ slightly. When I get to the final blessing, of having been granted life, sustained, and enabled to reach this moment, I look up and around while singing. The prayer is immediate and meaningful here, now more than ever.

Tuesday, September 11th, 2018 10:25 AM

I head out of my house fifteen minutes early to catch the cab to work. When I reach the corner, I get a text that it will be there in twenty-four minutes. It arrives in three. For Rosh Hashanah, the radio in the cab is playing a pop station's annual countdown of each year's top local hits. The streets are even more empty than on the Sabbath. A few women in skirts and long sleeves walk with carriages and strollers. Their husbands are probably still attending the long morning services for the holiday. A scattering of other people in swimming garb head for the beach. Signs on the street celebrate the new year. People who want to worship, worship. People who want to party, party. Except for those of us working in understaffed service positions, everybody looks relaxed.

Wednesday, September 12th, 2018 3:59 AM

From a distance, the girl appears to be walking on prosthetics. As I get closer, I see that she is on roller skates, possibly for the first time. She clutches the arm of a grey-haired man who also holds her far shoulder as they proceed down the sidewalk. The girl's feet slide around, their motion only vaguely related to the path that the rest of her body is taking. A woman on an electric scooter whips past them. She crouches, tilts, and stands as if she were surfing a massive wave on the level ground. A man runs by in the other direction, waving wildly at a bus that is pulling away. The bus slows but doesn't stop. The driver points to another, far less crowded bus from the same line that is pulling up behind him.

Thursday, September 13th, 2018 5:40 AM

A woman is shouting something about police and electricity. Looking past her, I see what she means. A boy on an electric bicycle has puttered past us, ignoring the sidewalk's clearly marked bike and scooter lanes. A cop gets in his way and escorts him to the curb, where a police car is waiting. They don't take him in, and I don't see them give him a ticket, but they do appear to check his ID and deliver a stern warning. He rides off, in the correct lane this time. As I pass the woman, she stops shouting and, sotto voce, asks for a few shekels. I apologize for not having any and move on.

Thursday, September 13th, 2018 9:48 PM

The pedestrian street is littered with something like grapefruit, though the skins are thinner and green. Each split open when it hit the ground. Each has been nibbled by unseen creatures. In my yard, fruit that looks on the outside like apples and on the inside like figs has fallen on the steps and furniture. The sweet odor of its decay greets me as I step out the door.

Friday, September 14th, 2018 **11:43 AM**

Children in yellow guards' vests are jeering at me in unison. Apparently, to let people cross the street on foot, they lower a long pole with a stop sign at the end. The one-handed "come hither" gesture wasn't meant for me, but for the car making a left turn that somehow managed not to hit me as I stepped off the curb.

Friday, September 14th, 2018 6:14 PM

The streets and stairs of this older city seem to smell of coconut. I gradually realize, though, that it's the scent of sunscreen from the person ahead of me on the walking tour.

Friday, September 14th, 2018 11:59 PM

In the square, women on a trap set and dumbeks drum along to tracks by Eminem.

Saturday, September 15th, 2018 12:20 PM

The elevator to the employee exit faces the beach, though the shore is several blocks away. As if in apology, there's a photographic mural of a shoreline on the wall as we come out, and the concrete steps to the outside are lined with astroturf. As I head out the door for the last time, I realize that I'd never gotten around to walking down to the beach after work. But it's close to midnight on the Sabbath, and my taxi is waiting.

On Sunday, I start a new job, working daytime hours, in the field in which I started, decades ago. Tuesday night and Wednesday are Yom Kippur. On Thursday, I'll be sixty years old. It's been a good year.

www.ingramcontent.com/pod-product-compliance
Lightning Source LLC
Chambersburg PA
CBHW071735150726
47998CB00005B/1653

9789659274208